INDIVIDUAL EDUCATION PLANS

IMPLEMENTING EFFECTIVE PRACTICE

Janet Tod

Frances Castle

Mike Blamires

David Fulton Publishers
London

David Fulton Publishers Ltd
Ormond House, 26–27 Boswell Street, London WC1N 3JD

First published in Great Britain by David Fulton Publishers 1998

Note: The right of Janet Tod, Frances Castle and Mike Blamires to be identified as the authors of this work has been asserted by them in accordance with the Copyright, Designs and Patents Act 1988

British Library Cataloguing in Publication Data
A catalogue record for this book is available from the British Library

ISBN 1–85346–520–8

Typeset by Textype Typesetters, Cambridge
Printed in Great Britain by Bell and Bain Ltd, Glasgow

Contents

Preface Page iv

Acknowledgements Page v

How to use this book Page vi

Introduction Page viii

Well, that about wraps it up for IEPs … or does it? Page 1

Individual Education Plans Page 11

	Principles	Institutional self-review	Ideas for action
IEPs (general)	Pages 26–7	Pages 28–30	Page 31
Assessment	Pages 32–6	Pages 28–30	Page 37
Targets and strategies	Pages 38–43 Pages 48–51	Page 44	Pages 45–7 Page 52
Monitoring	Pages 53–6	Page 57	Pages 58–9
Parental partnership	Pages 60–61	Pages 62–63	Page 64
Involving the learning and the peer	Pages 65–6	Page 67	Page 68
The role of outside agencies	Pages 69–70	Page 71	Page 72
Making use of IT with IEPs and administration	Page 73	Page 74	Pages 75–8

References Page 79

Appendices Page 81

Preface

This book has attempted to put forward a case for IEPs as part of a school's 'inclusive and effective practice' for the diversity of its pupils and the requirements of the Code of Practice.

We maintain that IEPs should be part of a whole-school response to special needs. We have tried to avoid hectoring schools into reluctant compliance with the *letter of the Code*.

We have also tried to encourage schools to build upon their existing good practice and respond to the underlying *principles of the Code*.

As this book goes to print, good practice with IEPs is developing further; this will be documented by the next books in this series.

Janet Tod
Frances Castle
Mike Blamires
May 1998

Acknowledgements

This book resulted from work undertaken as part of a research project commissioned by the DfEE and managed at the Special Needs Research and Development Centre of the Department of Education at Canterbury Christ Church College of Education.

The authors would like to express their thanks to teachers and officers in the following LEAs who contributed to the project. The views represented in this book are those of the authors and are not intended to represent the views or policies of any particular body or LEA.

East Sussex
Hampshire
Humberside
The Isle of Wight
Kent
The London Borough of Newham
The London Borough of Tower Hamlets
West Sussex
The Wirral

In particular, the team would like to acknowledge the contributions from:

Tom Brown, SENCO, Woodside School
Colin Hardy, SEN Advisory Teacher, The London Borough of Newham
Garry Hornby, University of Hull
Keith Humphreys, University of Northumbria
Kate Jacques, St Martin's College, Lancaster
Mike Kelly, SEN Advisory Teacher, The London Borough of Newham
Bonnie Mount, Secretary to the Special Needs Research and Development Centre
Miranda Preston, Chichester Institute of Education
Tanya Sealey, Clerical Support Assistant to the Project

How to use this book

The ideas and procedures contained in this book have been developed with practitioners in many different settings. The book is based on observations of current practice and recognises that schools will be at different stages of development and may have differing priorities and resources. The proposed review of the Code of Practice, and the response to the Green Paper on SEN, will be an opportunity for schools to reassess the effectiveness of their procedures in meeting the special educational needs of their pupils.

The format of the book reflects three key aspects of the development of IEP procedures. These are:

Principles

Following the publication of the Code of Practice many schools focused their efforts upon meeting the Code's administrative requirements for IEPs. Other schools responded to the underlying *principles* and adapted their existing good practice. This allowed them to have regard to the Code while at the same time developing procedures which were manageable given their particular circumstances. For example the IEP procedure as described in the Code has proved to be particularly challenging for some secondary schools and for schools with a relatively high number of pupils at Stage 2 of the Code and beyond. Each section of this book thus contains a section concerned with *principles* to be considered by a school in interpreting the Code.

School development via institutional self-review (ISR)

Effective schools have responded to the demands of the Code in general, and IEPs in particular, by integrating procedures into their school development planning. This has changed the perception of the Code from that of a set of prescriptions with the emphasis on individual rights and responsibilities into a document which informs and guides an ongoing process of collaborative school development for inclusive SEN provision. Schools are increasingly recognising the need to encourage shared responsibility for IEP procedures. Central to this is the developing role of parents, pupils, and outside agencies. The regular monitoring of the school's collective IEPs has enabled the targeting of resources. Each section of this book contains *an institutional self-review* (ISR) to enable schools to self-assess and develop their own action plans.

Ideas for action

Many schools have found that class and subject teachers need to be supported in developing skills beyond planning IEP target setting. Some schools are developing their own shared strategy banks, others are using strategies contained in published SENCO support packs as a starting point. A development which is becoming evident in schools is the increasing use of technology (e.g. World Wide Web) for the sharing and exchange of strategies for meeting SEN. One such on-line resource is the SEN Xplanatory (www.canterbury.ac.uk/xplanatory/xplan.htm) developed by Mike Blamires at the Special Needs Research and Development Centre.

Each section of the book contains some *ideas for action* for consideration. For example, the section on 'Assessment and Monitoring' seeks to illustrate how IEPs might be integrated into a school's general arrangements for assessment and recording the progress of all pupils. The sections address areas of particular relevance to IEP procedures.

To use this book the reader has to select the appropriate section from the contents page grid on page 1. This book is intended to provide a practical resource to schools. For example, if the SENCO has decided to delegate the setting of targets for IEP planning to class or subject teachers and needs to deliver a staff development activity, the section covering 'Principles of Target Setting' will provide a useful starting point.

Introduction

It was stated by Baroness Blatch in the House of Lords on 23 April 1993 that the Code of Practice '... will not impose duties ... the Code will promote good practice and will benefit children ...' Since the implementation of the Code of Practice (COP) in 1994 schools have been developing systems and strategies for the implementation of Individual Education Plans (IEPs) for pupils with special educational needs (SEN) as part of the Code and there has been a demand for published resources to support this activity.

However, it has recently been suggested that elements of the Code, and IEPs in particular, are isolating rather than including pupils (e.g. Ainscow 1997), and that they focus attention on individual pupils rather than on the learning environment (Greenhalgh 1996). Further, the Code has reinforced '... the meeting of special educational needs in terms of the identification and assessment of individuals rather than through a pro-active, whole school, curriculum based approach' (Greenhalgh 1996). This has been seen to encourage a deficit model based upon the child (Dyer 1995).

In its favour, the Code has raised teacher awareness of SEN and it has been '... the principal guide for improving the quality of education for pupils with SEN' (OFSTED 1997). This has not only been the experience of mainstream schools, as some special schools have found that IEPs have raised awareness and improved staff expertise (Rankin and Rees-Davies 1996).

The authors of this book attempt to place the IEP as part of the dynamic planning processes that shape a school's response to the educational needs of its pupils. We view the IEP as being an elaboration and refinement of existing practices for assessment and differentiation. The IEP is part of the progressive focusing and problem solving that enables entitlement to a broad and balanced curriculum for all of its pupils.

Well, that about wraps it up for IEPs ... or does it?

For IEPs to be developed effectively they have to be seen as 'worthy of the effort' by all involved. It is important for schools to be aware of the criticisms of IEPs and to be convinced of their need.

Could it be that IEPs are 'on their way out'?
How can the needs of the 'difficult to teach or vulnerable' be met to everyone's satisfaction if IEPs are no longer required?
Will these children vanish from the mainstream? If so will their 'normally expressive' parents be silenced?
Could this be another case for the X files...?

We took a look at some of the criticisms of IEPs and wondered what would happen if the case ever ended up in court.

The case for the prosecution

We call our first expert witness, Professor Dyson, who is a member of the DfEE SEN advisory committee and has had significant influence in the drawing up of the Green Paper on special educational needs. In a recent article he criticises individualisation:

> [The Code of Practice and Statementing] constitute a huge deployment of energy and resources into perpetuating the founding assumption of special education, namely that children's difficulties in school can be understood in terms of individual children's characteristics. They make it extremely difficult for policy-makers, managers and teachers to see those difficulties as generated by the nature of the education system and almost impossible for them to take the further essential step of locating the difficulties of individuals, and the shortcomings of schools, within broader socio-economic patterns of inequality and disadvantage.
>
> (Dyson 1997)

Dyson is suggesting that the individual consideration of special needs leads to the view of *within child* causes of special needs. This can negate the responsibility of teachers, schools and authorities to make educational responses to these needs. This individualisation also prevents schools from operating in the best interests of its pupils through the efficient use of limited resources. If underachievement is at the heart of special educational needs, then schools can best respond by targeting whole-school efforts to improve literacy and numeracy.

The case for the defence

Keefe makes a useful distinction between primary and secondary stakeholders in the education of children. She suggests that primary stakeholders are:

> ...the learners, parents and teachers, and they want information relevant to the learner's progress and instruction in the cognitive, affective and social domains. The secondary stakeholders may include school administrators ... and politicians, all of whom seek comparative data.
>
> (Keefe 1996)

The latter require data to compare schools and produce performance tables. Keefe notes that educational assessment usually responds to the needs of the latter group rather than the former. IEPs can redress this imbalance.

Sinason (1992) responds more bluntly to criticisms of individualisation: 'If we cannot bear to see when someone needs different provision verbally and practically we all end up being stupid.'

The case for the prosecution continues...

Dyson is further critical of the validity of extending the disability movement's pressure for inclusion to encompass underachievement.

> ...the concern to which the inclusion movement appears invariably to return is the right of disabled children to be placed in mainstream schools; an important issue, to be sure, but not one that is immediately relevant to the wide range of children experiencing educational difficulties who are already placed in the mainstream.
>
> (Dyson 1997, p. 155)

Whereas individualisation may be justified for pupils with physical or sensory needs, this principle has been inappropriately extended to learners whose difficulties have been *socially constructed*.

The case for the defence

From the defence case it appears that IEPs should only be appropriate for learners with 'physical needs' and not for those who are underachieving in the mainstream. Although this has some superficial appeal and fits with the current political climate, it assumes that these two categories are distinctive.

If this is accepted, there is a risk that we abandon the continuum of special needs by separating out disabilities from 'the educationally disadvantaged'. This is at odds with the Warnock Report (1978) which advocated dealing with educational need irrespective of causation.

There also appears to be a confusion between integration and inclusion. Integration is premised on conformity whereas inclusion is premised on diversity. If we adopt a model based on differing provision for different *causes* of need then it follows that teachers need to be skilled in identifying those pupils who will respond to whole-school approaches and those who need varying degrees ('the different and extra') of individualisation.

The case for the prosecution continues...

Professor Dyson suggests that individualisation has encouraged the construction of educational disabilities at the expense of responding to educational underachievement:

> emergence of the 'new disabilities' such as dyslexia, attention deficit disorder, dyspraxia and the various shades and forms of autism ... the discovery of such disabilities will have significant implications for special needs education as traditionally practised and understood.
>
> In particular, it seems likely that these changes are already shifting resources and attention away from whole-school responses to difficulties and disadvantage and towards provision for individual children. Moreover, it seems that the children who capture these resources are the ones whose parents are already so sufficiently well-resourced socially and financially that they can manipulate the education system to their children's interests.
>
> (Dyson 1997, p. 155)

The case for the defence

These 'new' or 'blue-chip' disabilities have, in fact, widened the consideration and expertise needed to address special needs. In some cases teachers have felt themselves deskilled in meeting the educational needs of these children. The fact that these disabilities are now emerging may be indicative of the lack of expertise teachers have had in recognising and responding to these needs. Many long-serving teachers on training courses in these areas often state that they came across these difficulties in children a long time before but did not have a framework for understanding and responding to them.

These 'new disabilities' may not really be that new. The Hadow Report of 1931 noted 'special disabilities, such as poor memory, unstable attention, poor visual or poor auditory imagery' and 'inherent emotional defects such as instability and emotional apathy'. (p.68) Could it be that the labels change but the children have always been there? Like 'the poor', children with these difficulties have always been with us.

It is false to assume that whole-school approaches to special needs are required to compete with meeting the needs of children with 'new disabilities'. In fact the Code seeks to marry progressive individualisation with whole-school responses.

> Schools need to give greater attention not so much to the specific details of the IEP, but to how it relates to the teacher's planning.
>
> (OFSTED 1997)

The implication that middle-class parents are exploiting the system for their own gain is not supported from evidence from studies of the economic status of parents who have taken their LEA to tribunal over lack of appropriate provision for their child (IPSEA 1997).

However, it might be that at lower levels of the Code, schools with catchment areas that are predominantly in the lower socio-economic groups are not effectively communicating the special needs policy to parents.

To criticise the involvement of parents and individualisation, could be construed as proposing a system that is designed according to the needs of the providers rather than the consumers (ACE 1997).

A provider-led approach has increased the numbers of school exclusions through the establishment of whole-school approaches to discipline and behaviour that stress compliance and 'zero tolerance' rather than negotiation with individual pupils. As the Elton report noted, whole-school behaviour policies will work with most pupils, however, something 'different and extra' is needed for the small proportion of pupils who are not served by this policy. Dwyfor Davies (1996) notes that '... there is an overwhelming desire on the part of children with EBD to negotiate individual learning programmes'. Where children with these difficulties have not been actively involved, there has been evidence that they have been isolated from the process and felt '... they were being "done to" rather than participating in'. The IEP can provide a framework for the 'real' negotiation that these learners desire.

The case for the prosecution

> The fashion has been in recent years to pillory schools in inner city areas and in economically depressed communities on the assumption that their problems must be generated by poor management and poor teaching ... Rather than condemning them, we should seek to understand how social and economic stresses in the schools' environments interact with the schools themselves to generate the problems of learning and behaviour which hit the newspaper headlines.
>
> (Dyson 1997, p. 156)

Professor Dyson goes on to suggest that these schools are being proactive in the face of their difficulties and see themselves as being engaged in a two-way interaction with the socio-economic environment in which they are located. These schools are also 'responding to the stresses and problems which are endemic within it and making a positive contribution to their alleviation'. Within this context it could be argued that individualisation is not cost-effective or necessary.

The defence responds

Shouldn't this really be a four-way interaction? The parents are in danger of being lost from the equation again along with the learners. Without their involvement the identification of 'stresses and problems which are endemic' (Dyson 1997) becomes a set of decisions based upon benevolent paternalism. The users of a system have to have a voice. The process of partnership inherent in Individual Education Plans and the Code of Practice is at the heart of leading-edge practice.

The first exhibit for the prosecution

The DfEE Green Paper 1997a: Excellence for all children: Meeting Special Educational Needs

> ...Schools have expressed concern about the cost of implementing the guidance in the Code and about the 'bureaucracy' resulting from it, particularly in relation to IEPs and annual reviews of statements. It has been suggested that, too often, attention is focused upon getting the paperwork right, at the expense of providing practical support to the child.
>
> (Chapter 3, Section 3)

Defence response

No one said it would be easy to meet the needs of these children. The current wisdom on IEPs is that they should be brief working documents that inform teaching (e.g. OFSTED 1997). Initially, much effort was focused on the paper format of IEPs with some IEPs being produced for accountability purposes rather than to help plan action. Some LEAs have strict criteria for the content of IEPs and forms to support their audit procedures which are then used to allocate funding for SEN to the school. Most SENCOs now have more streamlined IEP procedures which do not duplicate, but build upon existing systems of assessment and recording and are indicative of the school sharing the responsibility for meeting SEN.

Where schools and SENCOs are still complaining about 'paperwork' then a complete information strategy needs to be considered for the entire school as well as for meeting SEN. Such a strategy needs to take account of new technologies. SENCO time is an important resource which needs to be supplemented by IT and clerical support.

One of the key principles of the Code of Practice is that 'Schools should be accountable for their provision for learners with SEN'. The improvement in SEN practice that has been documented by OFSTED and other sources is largely due to schools' responses to the IEP's requirements. This pressure should not be let up.

Bring on the next expert witness for the prosecution: 'Calling Alan Goddard'

Alan Goddard recently wrote an extensive and damning critique of IEPs based upon work on both sides of the Atlantic:

> All IEPs are inextricably linked with a curriculum based on the behavioural objectives model... The model is linear, hierarchical and reductionistic, adopting a step by step approach to learning, and embracing a product ideology...
> ...There is now a major paradigm shift away from 'mechanistic reductionism' to 'holistic constructionism'.

IEPs not only dictate teaching methods (which emphasise teaching to a test, and tend to fragment authentic learning opportunities and experiences of pupils), but also encourage an assessment stance to the curriculum.

IEPs also isolate children from each other, inhibiting collaborative learning, and quell the child's initiative and independence, as he or she becomes dependent upon the teacher's requests.

If pupils are allowed to consider problems in their own way they might well be in a position of using their own unique means of making sense of the world.

(Goddard 1997)

The prosecution rests...

The defence presents its case

Some have applauded Goddard's critique as a warning of the dangers of Literacy and Numeracy hours which now dictate *how* children should be taught as well as content. There is a danger for all children of teaching 'to the tests'. If IEPs are written to support the acquisition of a narrow set of skills without a real confidence in their use or in their potential range of applications, then it is unlikely that they meet the criteria for 'educational effectiveness' for pupils at Stage 2 and beyond.

Much of Goddard's criticisms of IEPs are based on American examples. These are not the same as IEPs arising from the Code. The US IEP is much like a statement or annual review with strict legal guidelines for implementation whereas the IEP, within the Code of Practice, was intended as a brief proactive plan of action.

Keefe has been critical of the American IEP framework:

> The IEP is supposed to be an instructional guide but there have been studies which call this into question (e.g. Lynch and Beare 1990; Smith 1990).
>
> These studies indicate that the objectives stated in IEPs may not be relevant to the student's needs and thus may not be the focus of instruction.
>
> A possible reason for the mismatch between IEP objectives and instruction is that the assessment measures used to develop goals and document progress do not reflect either authentic learning tasks or students' actual achievements.
>
> ... It is possible to write an IEP more responsive to learner needs.
>
> (Keefe 1996)

This may be achieved by adopting the UK approach in which the IEP is a working document rather than a legal contract. The IEP may historically be based upon small steps approaches but in practice it has developed beyond simple reductionism.

Furthermore guidance on IEPs within England and Wales provides criteria to construct and evaluate IEPs which should not isolate the child but identify learner needs with appropriate responses:

So far as possible, the plan should build on the curriculum the child is following alongside fellow pupils and should make use of programmes, activities, materials and assessment techniques readily available to a child's teachers.

The plan should usually be implemented, at least in part, in the normal classroom setting.

(COP, 2:93)

Within the Code, the IEP is built upon the differentiation within the classroom to ensure that the child is offered entitlement to access a broad, balanced curriculum which is relevant.

The Code also stresses the advantages of involving the child.

The Benefits are:
Practical: children have important and relevant information. Their support is crucial to the effective implementation of any individual education plan.
Principle: children have a right to be heard. They should be encouraged to participate in decision making about provision to meet their special educational needs.

(COP, 2:35)

This is not at odds with Goddard's wishes to include the child but, despite the Code's rhetoric, the findings of OFSTED are that involvement seldom occurs. Where learners are involved in their IEPs, a number of advantages have been observed. Davie (1996) suggests that consulting and involving pupils is valuable in providing feedback. Black (1996) supports this, indicating that pupils' involvement can assist teachers in formative assessment, which he regards as 'in need of further development, if teachers are to know the state of their pupils' learning'. The capacity of pupils to judge their own work can be regarded as of fundamental importance to their learning. It is also suggested that they cannot play an effective part in their own assessment without a programme to sustain the objectives for their learning (Black 1996). OFSTED noted that schools which were efficient in meeting the requirements of the Code were those where 'Pupils' views of their own progress and difficulties were taken into account'.

The IEP can provide an effective framework which is meaningful to the learner.

The defence sums up

IEPs in isolation?

In order to respond to the diversity of learners, a school should have an 'accurate audit of needs' (OFSTED 1997). IEPs can provide this.

A consideration of a child's needs within an IEP should take into account the needs they share with others as well as the needs they share with a subgroup or with no one else. This can avoid Goddard's concern that targets will be narrow and isolate the child.

Norwich suggests three kinds of educational need which each child may have:

- individual needs;
  – arising from characteristics different from all others
  (a child may be the only child in the school with a particular learning style or sensory difficulty)
- exceptional needs;
  – arising from characteristics shared by some
  (a child may share certain learning characteristic or abilities with only some of his or her peers)
- common needs;
  – arising from characteristics shared by all
  (the need to belong, the need to feel safe, the need to have achievement and effort recognised)

(Norwich 1996)

From this, Cowne (1996) has posed some key questions for class and subject teachers to consider if they are going to be able to plan effectively for the children they teach (Figure 1). A teacher may only be confident in responding to these questions if whole-school systems of assessment and reporting are in place. Responding to the implications of these questions will require dynamic planning as described by Moore (1993) (Figure 1).

An initial and popular set of criteria for targets was that they should be SMART (Specific, Measurable, Achievable, Relevant, and Time related). However, this does not encourage alternative frameworks which are based upon the full range of curriculum opportunities that are available within a school. The National Literacy Targets (Figure 6) provide examples of SMART and non-SMART targets which are held to be worthwhile for all children.

A strong counter to the criticism that IEPs are too narrowly focused is the requirement for parental partnership. While some expectations of parents may be considered unrealistic, recognition of their hopes should ensure that the content of the IEP has relevance and application.

IEPs and inclusion

The Green Paper has brought a discussion of inclusion to the forefront of educational debate. The CEC (Council for Exceptional Children 1994) list twelve principles for successful inclusive schools. We list those where IEPs can be central to their achievement and practical management:

- an array of services that are coordinated across and among agency personnel
- systems for cooperation within the school: inclusive schools foster *natural* support networks across students and staff including peer tutoring, buddy systems, cooperative learning, co-teaching, team teaching and other forms of professional collaboration
- flexible roles and responsibilities
- partnership with parents.

Thomas, Walker and Webb suggest three further features of inclusion which we suggest would be aided by the use of IEPs:

- de-professionalisation: an inclusive school is one where there is an assumption amongst staff (shared by students) that all staff share in the contribution they make to children's learning
- democracy: an inclusive school is one in which all members – students, staff, parents and governors – share in the development and management of the school
- communication: in an inclusive school there is an assumption that all members will have a voice which will be heard and there will be systems for ensuring this voice is heard.

(Thomas, Walker, Webb 1997)

Finally

We can see the failings of narrow behavioural approaches in the past but note that implementation and evaluation criteria for educational effectiveness encourage IEPs that are in the context of curriculum entitlement.

The principle of shared ownership of IEPs means that a number of advocates are involved in the identification of the child's needs.

IEPs cannot compensate for all the negative effects of social-economic deprivation. IEPs can, however, address the educational consequences of this deprivation.

While most schools are still a long way from the ideal of inclusion, the IEP is central to the development of inclusive practices.

Meeting special needs at a classroom level
From differentiation to individualised planning
After Norwich (1996) and Cowne (1997).

Am I aware of the spread of needs of the pupils in my class?

Do I know the individual needs of the pupils in my class?

Do I know the strengths of my individual pupils?

What barriers to learning are there for these individuals to overcome?

Are all of these individual or some of these common?

How can I make my pupils feel safe enough to take risks in their learning?

How can I offer the whole balanced curriculum to these pupils without further reinforcing these barriers?

How can I ensure progress and positive self-esteem?

Figure 1

Individual Education Plans

What is an Individual Education Plan?

The term IEP refers to both a process and a document. The document serves two key purposes:

- *educational*: The IEP communicates the targets to be met and the anticipated learning outcomes to all involved in its delivery. The document triggers action. For example, for a parent of a child with a language delay this might simply be a diary in which they record their child's response to ten minutes daily additional input focused around a few targeted key subject words. This action, agreed with the SENCO, aims to support their child in developing understanding and usage of subject related topic words. By recording their child's response in a diary they monitor their part in the IEP and are able to provide summary information when it is reviewed. The same individual pupil would experience the class or subject teacher's action. Action might also be taken by a specialist from an outside agency such as a speech therapist. Each person involved in the delivery of the IEP is responsible for their own action and reports back summary information to the SENCO at times of review. Such a system reduces the detail that has to be written on the IEP. Action underpins the Individual Education Plan.
- *accountability*: The IEP acts as a summary document which provides evidence and evaluates the additional provision that has been allocated to the individual pupil. The IEP document is thus central to in-school and LEA review meetings. Schools need also to review their IEP documents so that school effectiveness in relation to SEN can be evaluated and areas highlighted for school development, budgeting and resource allocation.

Why do pupils need an Individual Education Plan?

Figure 2 illustrates the function of IEPs at Stages 2 and 3 of the Code. Clearly the function of IEPs is to allocate provision that is 'extra or different' to that at Stage 1. The IEP is not a compensatory device which makes up for lack of appropriate provision at Stage 1. The IEP forms part of the positive action planning process central to the Code and should signal the need for additional educational effort.

Figure 3 illustrates some of the perceptions of IEPs by teachers which have influenced IEPs' development.

The Advisory Centre for Education (ACE 1997) has noted that schools need to balance individual planning for pupils with SEN with whole-school planning to secure good standards of literacy, numeracy and behaviour, particularly when the school has a suitable number of pupils who are underachieving and where many have SEN. Head teachers and the SENCOs should ensure that IEPs are effective, manageable, and easily understood by parents, pupils, and staff.

Individual needs may be considered to have arisen from factors within the individual, their family, the school curriculum, the school environment, their socio-economic

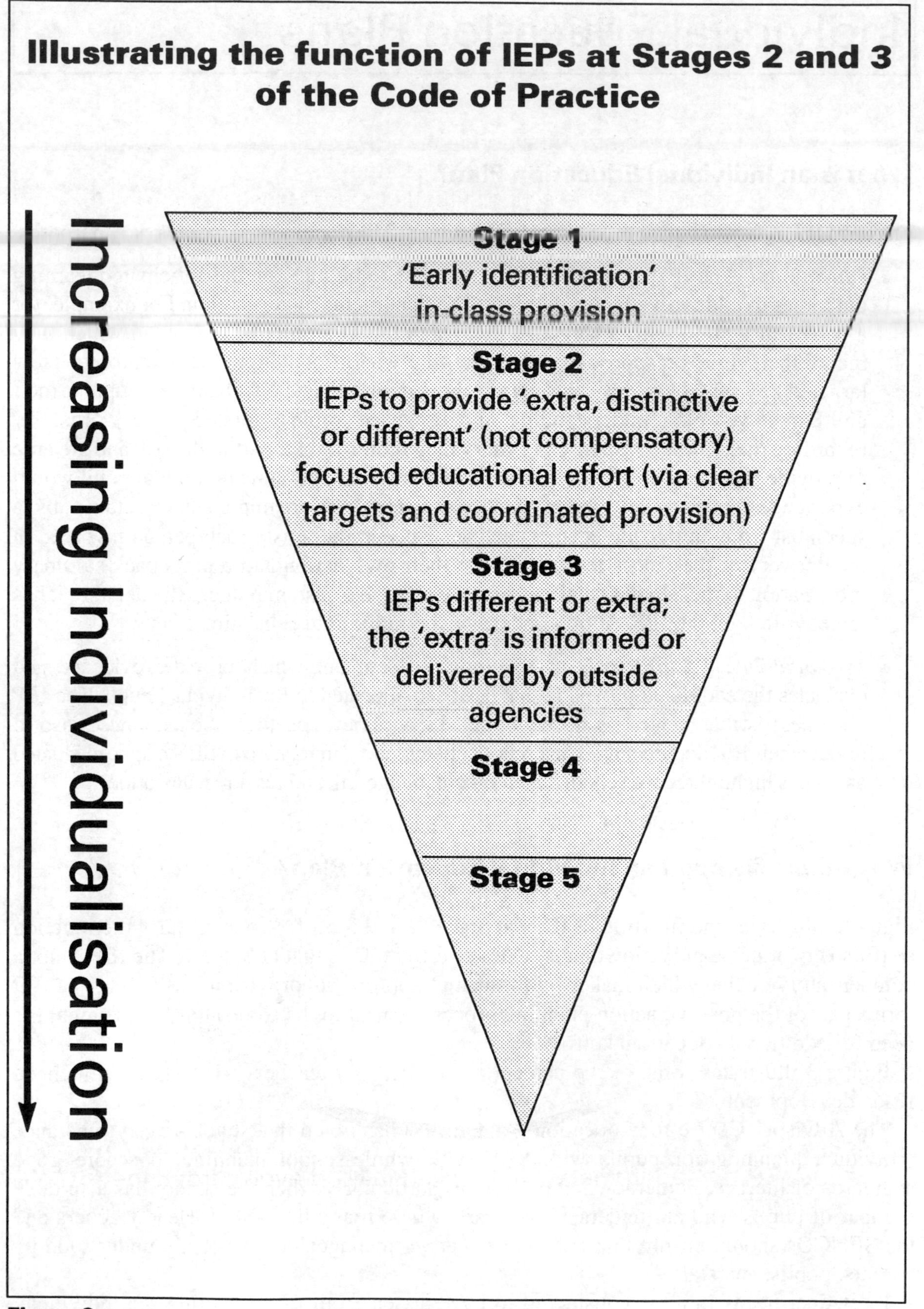

Illustrating the function of IEPs at Stages 2 and 3 of the Code of Practice
Increasing Individualisation
Stage 1
'Early identification' in-class provision
Stage 2
IEPs to provide 'extra, distinctive or different' (not compensatory) focused educational effort (via clear targets and coordinated provision)
Stage 3
IEPs different or extra; the 'extra' is informed or delivered by outside agencies
Stage 4
Stage 5

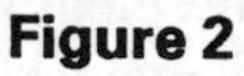
Figure 2

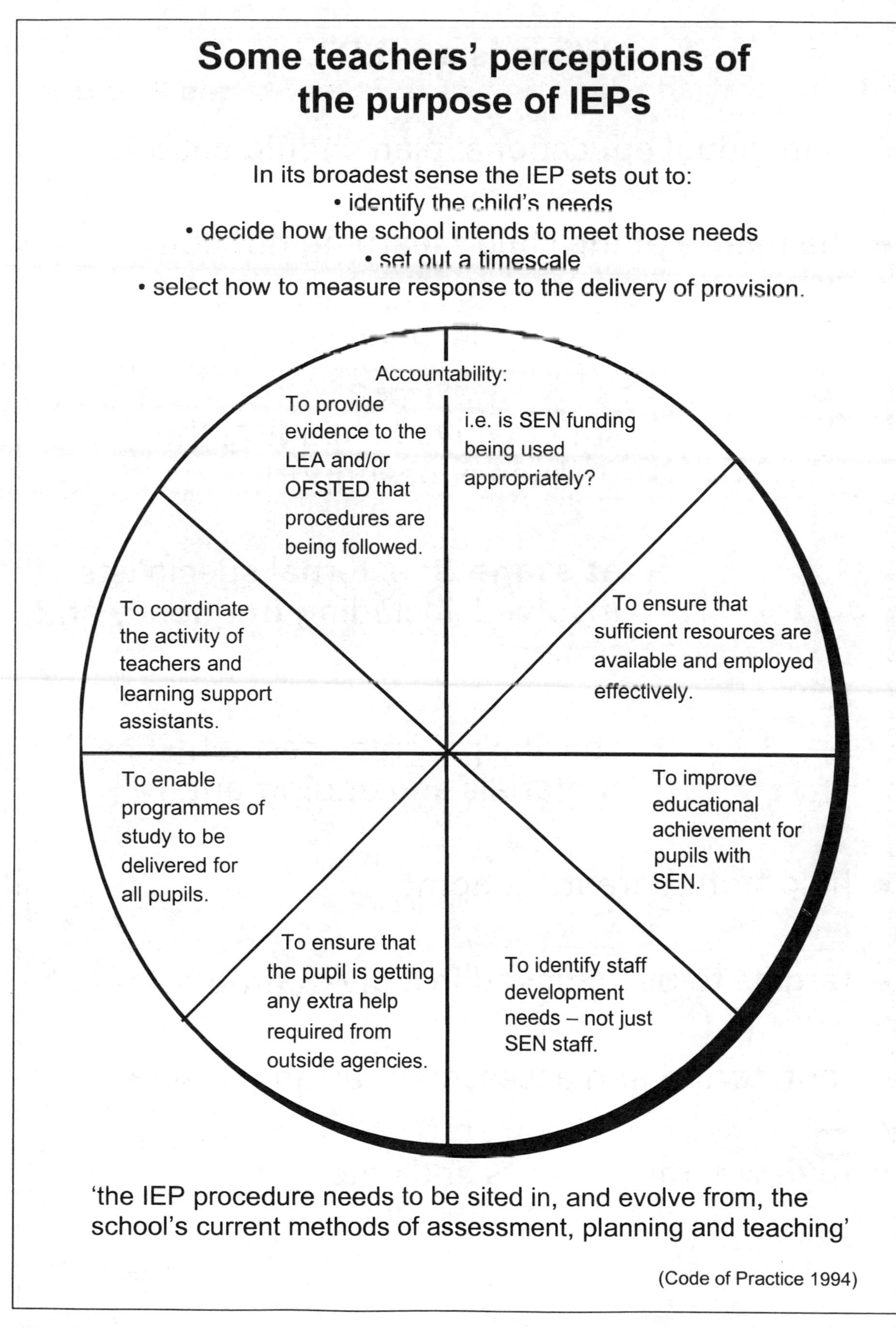
Some teachers' perceptions of the purpose of IEPs
In its broadest sense the IEP sets out to:
• identify the child's needs
• decide how the school intends to meet those needs
• set out a timescale
• select how to measure response to the delivery of provision.
Accountability:
To provide evidence to the LEA and/or OFSTED that procedures are being followed.
i.e. is SEN funding being used appropriately?
To ensure that sufficient resources are available and employed effectively.
To improve educational achievement for pupils with SEN.
To identify staff development needs – not just SEN staff.
To ensure that the pupil is getting any extra help required from outside agencies.
To enable programmes of study to be delivered for all pupils.
To coordinate the activity of teachers and learning support assistants.
'the IEP procedure needs to be sited in, and evolve from, the school's current methods of assessment, planning and teaching'
(Code of Practice 1994)

Figure 3

What is an IEP?

An individual educational plan should set out:

- the nature of the child's learning difficulty
- action
  - the special needs provision
  - staff involved including the frequency of support
  - **at stage 3:** external specialists involved, including frequency and timing
  - specific programmes/activities/materials and equipment
- help from parents at home
- targets to be achieved in a given time
- monitoring and assessment arrangements
- review arrangements and date

(Code of Practice 2:93)

OHP 1

environment or a combination of all these factors. The IEP procedure was developed in recognition of the fact that some pupils with SEN needed to have educational effort clearly focused towards meeting a few clearly defined targets irrespective of the complexities of attributed causation. *The IEP was designed to be additional to and not instead of other SEN provision provided by the school.*

> at the core of the Code's endorsement of the IEP lies a simple idea: if an institution or group of people gather their efforts round one or more straightforward objectives and review, after a specified time, whether these objectives have been achieved the desired change is more likely to take place.
>
> (SCAA 1995)

In the case of Stage 3 IEPs, this includes additional outside agencies. Figure 4 represents the different educational components of an IEP for a pupil with difficulties in reading. The grid represents a concept of an IEP rather than a grid to be filled. On the right is the curriculum described in 'key skills' to ensure that targets are curriculum linked. At the top are the pupil's needs based on the idea of 'different or extra' (this is a relative concept depending on teacher expertise at Stage 1). These needs are translated into targets. The left-hand side of the grid directs attention to the roles and responsibilities of all those involved in meeting the targets.

Many schools recognise that IEPs have been helpful in:

- providing a vehicle for the development of collaboration and involvement with parents, and a mechanism for enabling pupils to become more involved in their own learning plans
- directing teacher attention towards the setting, and resetting of clear, educationally relevant targets
- involving staff in the development and implementation of strategies to meet those targets, thereby improving and sharing classroom practice
- harnessing available resources to meet those strategies
- increasing the emphasis on the monitoring of pupil response to teaching
- providing clearer evidence as to the effectiveness of additional SEN provision.

How are schools developing their response to IEP procedures?

Schools and LEAs have made considerable efforts to comply with the IEP procedures described in the Code. However the pressures on SENCOs has been well documented and there is a clear need to develop systems and strategies to reduce this pressure while still adhering to the principles of provision embodied in the IEP procedures. The initial emphasis was on developing the IEP format, based presumably on the hope that if the paperwork could be solved then the process would follow. This has been gradually replaced by concerns for developing strategies which support the actual delivery, monitoring and evaluation of the IEP.

> In many schools a large proportion of the SENCO's time is given to writing and reviewing IEPs, often at the expense of enabling the SENCO to work with individual pupils. Some SENCOs, however have found that the training in the writing and reviewing

English – Reading *Opportunities for improving learning*	Alternative presentation of written material	Increased experience with the format and structure of books	Emphasis on rhyme and segmentation of words	Use of multimedia reading techniques	Emphasis on prediction and scanning initial letter sounds	Individual dictionary with pictures	Emphasis on skills involving syllabific action	Encouragement to make books for younger pupils	Extra systematic look, cover, write and check strategies	Emphasis on reading for meaning – not reading aloud	Opportunitiesa for over learning of phonic strategies in class	Over learning of core vocabulary or sight words	The Educational components of an IEP for a pupil with reading difficulties *Key Skills*
Whole Class													Conventions of language: developing an understanding of grammatical structure, patterns of language and presentational devices; talking about books; using correct terminology
Group													Vocabulary: recognising a wide range of words and applying this knowledge to reading unfamiliar words and phrases
Peer/Pair													Phonological awareness: recognising the relationship between print symbols and sound patterns; reading aloud with fluency and accuracy
C.A./ Support													Purpose and use of reading: understanding the nature and the many purposes of reading; reading a variety of materials
Individual Pupil													Contextual understanding: understanding meaning derived from the text as a whole; discovering meaning beyond the literal; distinguishing fact from opinion and recognising how writer expresses viewpoint in presentation, attitude and assumptions
Home/ parent													Paraphrasing: re-telling or re-presenting stories or information
Specialist Support (i.e. Speech & Language Therapist)													Response to reading: showing imaginative and intellectual responses to reading; engaging in critical thinking and showing a sound use of inference, deduction, reference and evaluation; selecting relevant information and comparing and synthesising two or more texts; expressing own opinion using the text as a solid reference point
Other outside agencies													Organising information: using structural materials for organising information and looking at different ways of reading, e.g. scanning; using references material such as library classification systems, catalogues and indexes, dictionaries, thesauruses and glossaries; looking at the way books can be adapted to other media

Figure 4

of an IEP is a highly effective way of providing in-school SEN training for other teachers and support staff.

(OFSTED 1997 6:68)

Schools have responded in various ways which include:

Phased introduction

Many schools seem to have been going through a similar process in implementing IEPs at whole-school level. This could be summarised in a series of steps:

Step 1: An IEP format is initially designed in order to meet perceived legislated requirements. This is either a pilot or becomes implemented (sometimes published formats are customised or LEA models are used).

Step 2: The format is reviewed in the light of experience gained at Stage 1 (this usually involves a simplification) and taking into consideration how class/subject teachers, parents and pupils can become active participants in the procedure.

Step 3: Schools examine how IT might serve to lessen the burden of the repetitive paperwork involved in IEP recording. They also look at systems to help monitor IEPs.

Step 4: Concern becomes focused on the actual educational effectiveness of the procedure. Enthusiasm for responding to the challenge of IEPs has been tempered by the recognition that the monitoring and evaluation of the educational effectiveness of IEPs is based upon developing practice in whole-school procedures in assessment and planning.

Schools may recognise which step they are on. Many are already at step 4. Some primary schools feel that they have IEPs fully in place and have received praise from OFSTED. Other schools have found it difficult to make a difference between Stage 2 ('different' and 'extra') and Stage 3 ('different', 'extra' and 'specialist'). In some areas of the country there is little outside specialist support available so that Stage 3 in effect does not exist.

Some schools have decided to report on pupil progress three times per year (two short reports, one more detailed). By this process the results of termly reviews of IEPs can be integrated into the report, communicated to parents, and targets set and agreed by parents signing and returning the report.

Two schools reported that they had decided to introduce IEPs for *all* pupils to ensure that SEN/IEPs were integrated into the fabric of the school Many schools are working on improving their policies and practices for parental involvement so that the IEP procedures are supported. The use of IT to generate IEP documents, letters to parents and other paperwork is becoming increasingly evident in schools. This 'phasing in' and modifying of procedures has led schools to accept that the implementation of IEPs is an ongoing developmental process which needs to be both manageable and managed.

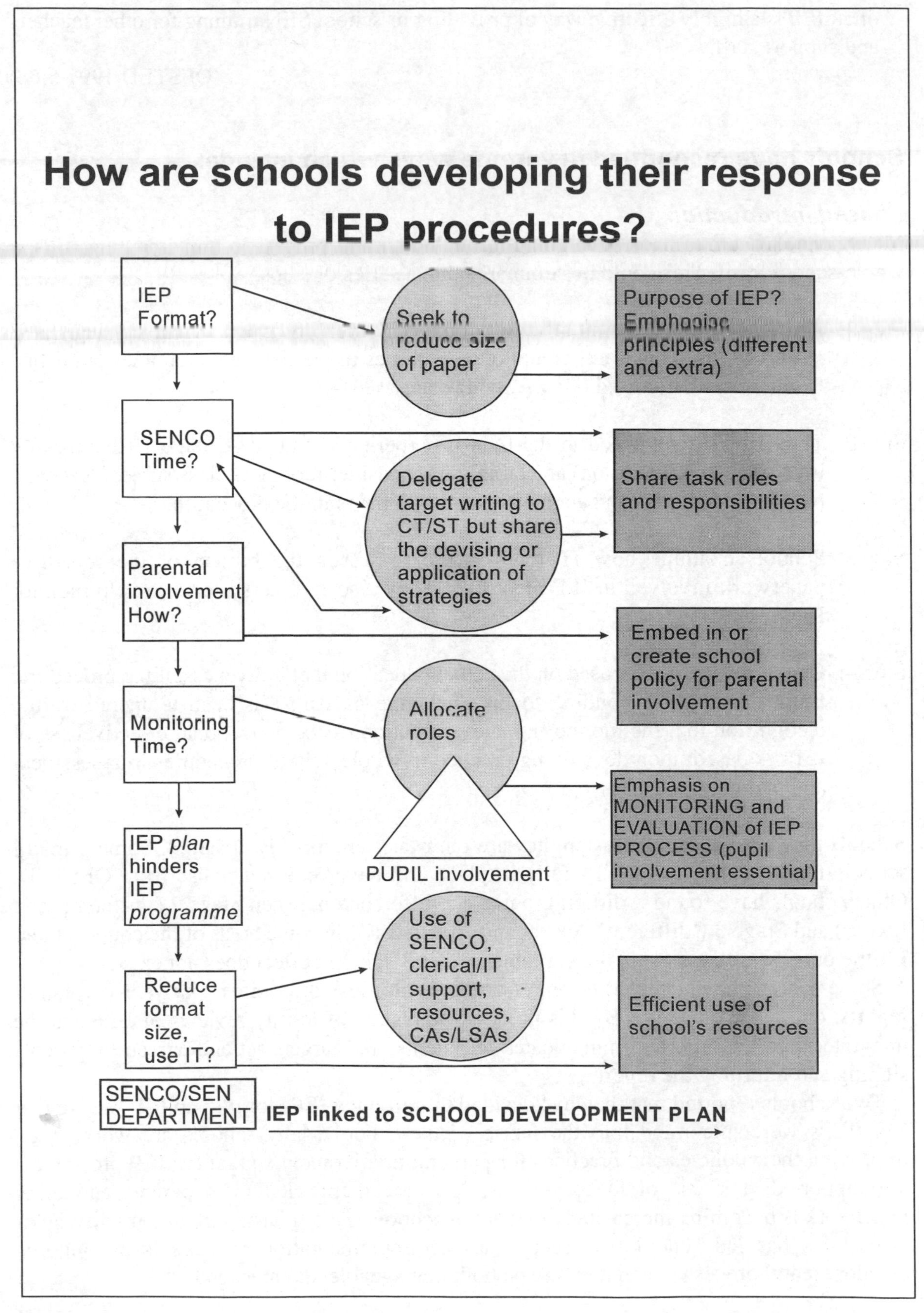
How are schools developing their response to IEP procedures?
IEP Format?
Seek to reduce size of paper
Purpose of IEP? Emphasise principles (different and extra)
SENCO Time?
Delegate target writing to CT/ST but share the devising or application of strategies
Share task roles and responsibilities
Parental involvement How?
Embed in or create school policy for parental involvement
Monitoring Time?
Allocate roles
PUPIL involvement
Emphasis on MONITORING and EVALUATION of IEP PROCESS (pupil involvement essential)
IEP plan hinders IEP programme
Use of SENCO, clerical/IT support, resources, CAs/LSAs
Reduce format size, use IT?
Efficient use of school's resources
SENCO/SEN DEPARTMENT
IEP linked to SCHOOL DEVELOPMENT PLAN

OHP 2

Simplifying and reducing the amount of paperwork

This has been consistently reported as the biggest problem. Schools want common procedures for IEPs that are manageable and effective. As a consequence, there must be time available to deliver and monitor IEPs. If SENCOs' time is taken up with clerical tasks, this is not an effective use of human resources. SENCOs have sought to reduce the paperwork but the Code does require that certain information must be recorded, and some LEAs have specified the amount of detail that must be recorded by the introduction of standard formats. Any attempt to reduce the amount of information needed on IEPs is also constrained by the fact that the IEP does have an accountability function.

However, if the paperwork is impeding the actual delivery of the IEP then the purpose of the whole procedure comes into question. Some schools have sought to reduce the paperwork by developing 'tick sheet' formats for defined SEN categories e.g. speech and language difficulties, emotional and behavioural difficulties, so that teachers can select and tick targets from a given range, tick strategies, and circle those staff involved in the procedure. Most schools have aimed to reduce the IEP format to one page. (An example of such an IEP format which is brief and allows for regular monitoring is included on the following pages.) The updating of IEPs has sometimes been achieved by the 'low tech' means of attaching the revised targets to the original formats by 'post-it' notes or stapled cards. To date SENCOs have sought to reduce their paperwork by:

- delegating clerical tasks to administrative staff; these staff take responsibility for the administrative IEP functions such as collating information, distributing IEPs, arranging review meetings etc. Such a strategy is cost-effective in that it releases the SENCO to contribute her expertise to supporting the educational function of the IEP.
- delegating Stage 2 IEPs to class teachers and form tutors; the SENCO then supports teaching staff in writing targets and strategies and devolves the responsibility for monitoring to all those involved in the IEP procedure, including the pupil where appropriate. Some schools have a person responsible for SEN in each subject area. Subject SEN coordinators liaise with, and are supported by, the school SENCO and are responsible for ensuring that pupils who have IEPs are appropriately supported.
- the use of IT support;
- supporting classroom assistants in specified areas of SEN so that they become more skilled in the delivery and monitoring of IEP procedures;
- the development of brief IEPs that only contain brief summary information referring to provision and procedures which are documented elsewhere (e.g. teacher planners, LSA workbooks);
- supporting the use of 'Group IEPs' for pupils who have similar needs in an attempt to reduce paperwork; while the term 'Group *Individual* Education Plan' is a conceptual anomaly, the practice of delivering what might be better termed a 'Group Learning Plan' has served to reduce paperwork and increase in-class individuali*sed* provision. An exemplar is in the appendix. Pupil response to such a plan has to be assessed on an individual basis. Another point of view would suggest that such an approach negates the use of the Code's stages which were intended as a progressive focusing upon individual needs. It might also encourage inflexible grouping or a sink class. The use of IT resources with the ability to cut and paste might replace the practice of Group IEPs with template IEPs that can be easily configured to individuals.
- increased involvement of parents in the IEP procedure; paradoxically, this can ease the workload by making the IEP more worthwhile for the pupil.

One other key strategy for reducing the paperwork is for schools to seek to reduce the number of pupils for whom they have to provide 'different or extra' provision – that is reduce the number of IEPs. Additional targeted, monitored provision at Stage 1 and above to meet the needs of particular SEN groups described by the school's SEN register could serve to provide effective provision and reduce the number of pupils who need individual targeted support at Stage 2 of the Code and beyond.

A possible definition of the function of the SENCO is to work proactively at a whole-school level and beyond to ensure that as *few learners as possible* need to be placed on the school's SEN register and as *many learners as possible* are enabled to be taken off the register.

Ongoing concerns arising from developing practice

- The views of the pupils themselves are rarely sought in the preparation of IEPs or in the review process even though the Code of Practice strongly recommends this (OFSTED 1997 2:15).
- The transfer of IEP information, as well as SEN records generally, between schools is a weakness.
- IEP planning often does not operate effectively alongside the school's literacy policy (OFSTED 1996 2:11) and we suspect that this will be the case for numeracy also. This leads to the issue of how IEPs can be linked in with the new literacy and numeracy hours in primary schools.
- Target setting could result in a narrowing of experience for SEN pupils and a decrease in their entitlement to access a broad and balanced curriculum.
- IEPs may be used as evidence of failure in an attempt to secure additional resources.
- Classroom assistants are used increasingly to deliver programmes prescribed by outside agencies (e.g. speech and language therapists, occupational therapists etc).
- The IEP procedures may not be working effectively for pupils with emotional and behavioural difficulties.

Should there be a standard IEP format?

> Most LEAs, as part of their INSET on the Code, and in their handbooks, have provided guidance about the content and purpose of IEPs. Where they have been more specific and tried to produce and encourage the use of standardised IEPs schools have found these too prescriptive, too detailed, and consequently often impossible to complete and review. Where LEAs have not encouraged a standardised approach many SENCOs and schools have appealed for them to do so. This is becoming a dilemma for LEAs and schools.
>
> (OFSTED 1996)

> Schools have usually followed the LEA format for writing but some have devised their own. Where this has happened it has often been the result of staff discussions and training within the school and in some cases in collaboration with SENCOs from neighbouring schools. In such instances these home-produced IEP formats are often more manageable than those presented by LEAs.
>
> (OFSTED 1997)

An example of an IEP which could be used in the primary or secondary setting

The detail is limited to essentials for monitoring collective IEPs. The tear off signed slip serves to trigger those involved. The IEP is sent to all those involved and evaluated by the check list on the reverse.

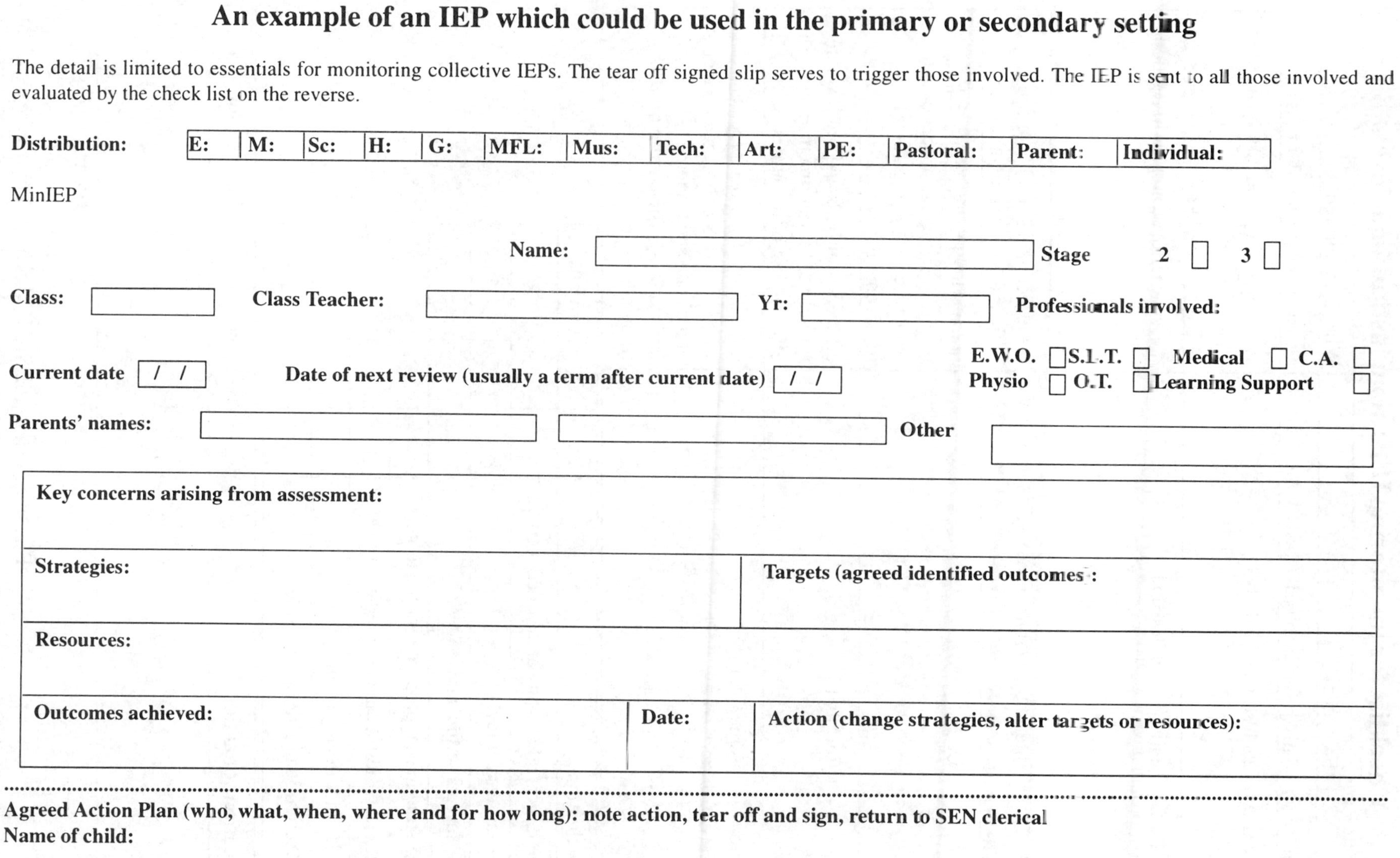

Distribution:

E:	M:	Sc:	H:	G:	MFL:	Mus:	Tech:	Art:	PE:	Pastoral:	Parent:	Individual:

MinIEP

Name: **Stage** 2 ☐ 3 ☐

Class: **Class Teacher:** **Yr:** **Professionals involved:**

E.W.O. ☐ **S.L.T.** ☐ **Medical** ☐ **C.A.** ☐
Physio ☐ **O.T.** ☐ **Learning Support** ☐

Current date / / **Date of next review (usually a term after current date)** / /

Parents' names: **Other**

Key concerns arising from assessment:		
Strategies:	**Targets (agreed identified outcomes):**	
Resources:		
Outcomes achieved:	**Date:**	**Action (change strategies, alter targets or resources):**

....

Agreed Action Plan (who, what, when, where and for how long): note action, tear off and sign, return to SEN clerical
Name of child:

Signature **Role e.g. teacher, parent, subject or special support** **Date:**

Checklist for monitoring IEPs at an institutional level

Role	Frequency	What is monitored?
Learner	daily [ ] on each task [ ]	e.g. success, difficulty of task
L.S.A. / C.A.	each session [ ] daily [ ]	self-help skills, motivation and time on task; response to strategy
C.T./S.T.	daily [ ] each lesson [ ]	e.g. success of strategies in relation to targets
SENCO	checking and sampling (state when)	the effectiveness of the design and delivery of the IEP
Outside Agencies	intermittent (state when)	the effectiveness and take-up of their advice and intervention
Parents	Daily [ ] Weekly [ ]	home school links, homework, rewarding progress at school and learner response to parental involvement
S.M.T.	Termly [ ]	efficiency of IEPs and implications for School Development Plan; efficient use of resources
Governors	Annually [ ]	goodness of fit of IEP procedures within the SEN policy; requirements of the code and resource implications; efficient use of resources

IEP Evaluation	Yes	No	Partially
Are the targets addressing areas of concern?			
Are the targets achievable?			
Are the targets setting challenges?			
Are the strategies appropriate for the targets?			
Are the strategies being delivered effectively?			
Is regular monitoring taking place?			
Is the Action Plan/IEP manageable?			

Implication for action	Action to be taken	By whom

Signed: Date:

Please return to the SENCO/Clerical by the review date

> Schools are, however, often persuaded or encouraged to use the LEA's format as this is seen to be more helpful where pupils are being considered for Stage 4 assessment. There can be a conflict here between devising and using a format seen as suitable for school use and a format of benefit for the LEA with a different purpose in mind.
>
> (OFSTED 1997)

The above quotations are indicative of the confusion and frustration that has been caused by IEP paper formats. They are caused by differing requirements for formative and summative record keeping which should be met through the use of an appropriate IT based assessment and reporting strategy for the whole school. This would mean that information can be collated and produced in a range of formats on a 'need to know' basis. The piece of paper is not the IEP but it could have been a red herring.

Rather than common formats for IEPs, common ways of recording agreed content have been found useful in aiding a pupil's transition between schools, and from school to post-compulsory education. Many schools have noted the difficulty of obtaining IEP information from some of their feeder schools.

At the heart of the debate concerning formats is the notion that 'the format' will somehow enable the procedure to be implemented.

> Schools are worried and confused over the way in which IEPs are used by inspectors and officers for purposes of accountability. There is sometimes a feeling that they need to be polished documents to withstand legal scrutiny rather than a practical basis for individualising planning. These worries have led some SENCOs to lose sight of the purpose of individual education plans. IEPS are successful where they promote effective planning by teachers and assist pupils to make progress through the setting and reviewing of particular learning targets. In addition they help to focus the teaching which enables pupils to achieve higher standards and have further learning opportunities. Schools need to give greater attention, not so much to the specific details of the IEP, but to how it relates to the teachers' planning.
>
> (OFSTED 1997)

The IEP should be worth more than the paper it is written on!

It may be useful for schools to view the IEP procedure as involving:

- A *document* which is placed on record as the IEP.
- A series of *monitored actions* informed from the IEP document. These are owned and recorded by teachers, parents, pupils and specialists etc.
- A *record card (pupil IEP)* which may be owned and carried around by the pupil to record action which has been taken. This 'record' may be written in the pupil's workbook.

The IEP format has to an extent been standardised by the fact that the Code has prescribed what it must contain. The amount of detail is influenced by what needs to be conveyed to those involved.

A simple IEP that conforms to the Code at Stage 2 could be:

Nature of child's learning difficulties: Emotional and Behavioural Difficulties.

People involved: (by name): Class teacher, learning support assistant, midday supervisors, parents, pupil.

Strategies and programmes: Via agreed Monitored Action Plans for all personnel.

Targets:

- will be able to work cooperatively for a minimum 5 minutes per day on a structured task with all adults involved in the IEP
- will demonstrate that he is able to increasingly seek attention from adults in a way which does not harm or disrupt others
- will demonstrate that he is able increasingly to play a structured turn-taking game with a peer or sibling while being supervised in an unstructured setting (playground and home)

Monitoring: Daily and weekly (to set sub-targets in relation to 'increasingly' (these may vary).

Review date: Termly.

(In this case all concerned have agreed what they are going to do to achieve the targets. This, and the child's response, will be recorded in the class teacher's planner, in learning support assistant's monitoring diary, in the midday supervisor's logbook, and in a parental and pupil diary.)

There are within- and between-school variations in the amount of information needed to be conveyed to individuals involved in any particular IEP. A standard format is unlikely to facilitate good practice.

Twelve key points for the implementation of IEPs

1. Schools can only develop IEPs from where they are now. A phased approach within the School Development Plan for SEN is vital.
2. In the long term IEPs must be concerned with the application of interventions which are different or extra and do not serve to simply document what should be occurring during earlier stages of the Code.
3. The administrative requirements of IEPs should not hinder the efficiency of the IEP in delivering appropriate provision.
4. IEPs bring to bear the strategies and resources that a school is able to harness in order to meet the needs of the learner with an IEP.
5. Targets should reflect the wide range of learning opportunities within the school. They should not be purely curriculum based or SMART.
6. The parental contribution to IEPs needs to be extended as part of a developing policy on parental partnership.
7. Learners need to be facilitated to take more responsibility for their own contribution to their IEPs to the extent that they are able.
8. IEPs need to be monitored by all those involved in order to ensure that documented provision is being delivered appropriately. This may occur at different times to different degrees as an extension of existing monitoring procedures.
9. It is likely that schools will need to examine the role of the SENCO so that they can coordinate special needs activities efficiently through the selective delegation of functions to SMT, teachers, classroom assistants and clerical support staff.
10. The paper requirements of IEPs can be extensive. It is highly appropriate to harness technology in the handling of this. The technology needs to be compatible with existing information strategies within the school, other agencies and the LEA. Sharing of information pertinent to IEP development will be facilitated as institutions become linked through the National Grid for Learning.
11. The contribution of outside agencies should serve to meet the targets set within the IEP.
12. Training and resource needs should follow from an evaluation of the current effectiveness of IEP procedures.

IEPs (general): Principles

Effective IEPs have the following characteristics:

- They are designed specifically for the individual child, taking into consideration age, ability, and past experience.
- They involve parental support and contribution.
- They include input from the child as far as possible.
- They have clear and relevant targets, focused on achievable goals.
- They are linked to the whole curriculum.
- They allow for the efficient use of resources.
- They are manageable.
- They increase learning opportunities for pupils with SEN.
- They are part of the School Development Plan for raising educational attainment for all pupils.
- They address both long-term and short-term aims.
- They trigger action plans which map clear roles and responsibilities for all concerned.

Educational *effectiveness* may have to be balanced with administrative compliance. For example, a detailed IEP which conforms to guidelines but which does not lead to real (observed) improved provision, is less effective than a shorter action-based document which delivers something *extra or different* for the pupil. However some LEA requirements may be useful in providing criteria for IEP effectiveness.

What teachers like about IEPs

IEPs:

- provide a focus for collaborative 'educational effort'
- enable all involved to share common goals via target setting
- provide an opportunity for staff development
- provide motivation to increase parental and child involvement
- provide a system for monitoring progress
- can be a vehicle for establishing procedures and systems for raising attainment for all pupils.

Possible difficulties

Teachers have identified the following:

- The *written* IEP is not translated into practice. It thus becomes a cumbersome paperwork exercise which results in little educational benefit for the pupil.
- If the SENCO takes on a major administrative role then his/her expertise in SEN teaching and coordination is not being effectively used.
- The IEP procedure is at risk of being used as an instrument for securing increased resources via 'evident failure'. This has been termed the 'perverse incentive'
- An adherence to an objectives model of teaching via the writing of clear targets (SMART) may lead to a narrowing of learning opportunities for SEN pupils.
- The simplification of the IEP procedure via checklists, strategy banks and the use of commercial IEP schemes could lead back to remediation via deficit rather than addressing individual needs.
- Difficulties in monitoring effectiveness of IEPs are such that there is a risk that IEPs will remain static documents or become so simplified that the educational benefit is questionable.

IEPs (general): Institutional self-review

Schools may find it helpful to examine their IEPs by using the checklists on the following pages.

The first page could be the focus of a staff development day devoted to the review of existing IEP formats.

The following page is a checklist that may be useful for a small school or a department.

An examination of responses to these self-review checklists will enable school to identify and prioritise future action.

Institutional self-review form for the IEP

The IEP itself:	Yes	Don't know	No
• Does the IEP chart progress from recognisable baselines?	☐	☐	☐
• Is it delivered in the context of curriculum entitlement?	☐	☐	☐
• Is it manageable?	☐	☐	☐
• Can it be regularly monitored?	☐	☐	☐
• Does it ensure an increase in learning opportunities for the SEN pupil?	☐	☐	☐
• Does it seek a partnership with the child and parents?	☐	☐	☐
• Does it map clear roles for all involved?	☐	☐	☐
• Does it state what is different or extra?	☐	☐	☐
• Does it ensure good practice in intervention conforming to LEA/national requirements?	☐	☐	☐
• Does it specify clear, achievable, educationally relevant targets?	☐	☐	☐
• Does it contain clear criteria for success?	☐	☐	☐
• Does it fit with the School Development Plan for raising pupil attainment?	☐	☐	☐
• Does it inform the allocation of resources?	☐	☐	☐
• Does it guide staff development needs in relation to SEN?	☐	☐	☐
• Does it identify strengths or weaknesses of the school's SEN policy?	☐	☐	☐
• Does it link into the school's systems for behaviour, assessment and differentiation?	☐	☐	☐

IEPs: Baseline institutional self-review

Self-evaluation exercise:

Has your department/school:

- integrated the assessment of SEN pupils into subject department assessment procedures for Stage 1 of the Code?
- acquired sufficient resources and skills and strategies to 'differentiate' at Stage 1?
- defined roles and responsibilities for those who currently contribute to the IEP procedure?
- enabled staff to set appropriate targets?
- developed subject based strategies for;

  Literacy targets?
  Behaviour targets?
  Subject specific targets?
  Numeracy?

- set up a system for staff to share effective strategies and resources?
- involved students in the setting of targets?
- involved those other than subject staff in planning programmes of work (e.g. SENCO, LSAs, pupils, parents)?
- developed a system of monitoring pupil response within IEP procedure which 'fits' with 'normal response to teaching' monitoring?
- made effective use of IT for IEPs and procedures?
- identified key subject skills linked to targets and strategies?
- developed targets and strategies for 'behaviour' which link with or extend the whole-school policy for behaviour?

Add any other key questions identified in discussion:

-
-
-

IEPs (general): Ideas for action

Strategies for implementation could include:

- The development of systems which seek to embed IEP procedures within existing school policies for planning, monitoring and self-evaluation and by using the appropriate Institutional Self review checklist.
- Simplifying documentation so that it is agreed and workable.
- The use of IT to archive all assessment information which can then be printed out in different formats on a 'need to know' basis.
- The gradual sharing of the workload by delegation of tasks to administrative, support and teaching staff, linked to appropriate training.

Assessment: Principles

> How can IEPs be integrated into the school's general arrangements for assessing and recording the progress of all pupils?
>
> (OFSTED 1996)

Problems experienced by schools in relation to assessment for the Code suggest that schools see this as an *additional* time-consuming task. Schools do in fact have considerable information about pupils but it is not always in a form that aids identification and planning.

SENCOs have reported difficulties when records:

- are only referred to when a pupil becomes a 'cause for concern' and are not used to inform forward planning. This is particularly relevant at transfer from primary to secondary school.
- are written in descriptive rather than evaluative terms and do not seek to address any specific questions such as 'what does this assessment information tell us about this pupil?' and 'how might we act on this information?'

Schools may consider that a useful development would be to support staff in reporting progress and needs so that this informs future planning.

Specific assessment requirements for the Code of Practice

- Assessment information for the Code needs to be interpreted and analysed – particularly assessment which records responses to specific interventions i.e. IEPs. Examining assessment information involves a process of problem solving which aims to inform the next stage of action – it is used for forward planning, not retrospective reporting.
- Summative assessment for the Code is prescribed to take place more frequently than the traditional yearly reports – normally reporting takes place termly to inform the next stage of action. Updating is thus a requirement which poses a particular challenge for those involved in IEPs as the original information cannot simply be erased and changed because it is needed for review meetings.

The challenge for schools is to ask themselves:

- What are our current assessment arrangements i.e. what information do we collect and at what intervals?
- How can we effectively extend or modify our existing assessment arrangements so that they support Code of Practice procedures?

Once this is established an action plan can be initiated which allocates roles and responsibilities and prescribes a time frame.

For the Code of Practice Stages 1–3, assessment may be considered to have three functions:

- assessment for planning (collaborative)
- assessment for monitoring (formative)
- assessment for evaluation (summative).

Figure 5 links COP planning for Stage 1 and Stage 2 and 3 IEPs by using the framework for curriculum planning described by SCAA (1995).

At Stage 1 assessment as described in the Code can be interpreted as seeking to answer the following questions:

- What are the *agreed* areas of concern for this pupil? This information is needed to decide what targets should be set.
- Under what conditions does the pupil learn/behave most effectively? This is addressed by collecting differing perceptions of the child and recording pupil strengths – the information can be used to decide upon strategies for meeting targets.
- What are the likely long-term aims for the pupil? This information can be gathered from establishing the 'wider context' of the child's learning difficulties.
- Which *resources* can be brought to bear to support pupil learning? This information is related to the 'wider context' of the child's learning difficulties, and concerns the degree of support currently available from parents, guardians, and outside agencies as well as the availability of in-school resources.

It follows that if procedures for the Code are going to be integrated into the school's existing procedures the SMT need to ask: 'Does the information that the school already collects for each pupil enable the above questions to be answered? If not what action needs to be taken?'

For Stages 2 and 3 of the Code, assessment might address the following questions.

	Question	Answer data	Action
Stage 1 Review Information	What progress has been made by the pupil at Stage 1 in relation to targets set?	Summary information from class teacher or year tutor. Minimum information could be 'good', 'satisfactory' or 'unsatisfactory'	If unsatisfactory: seek additional advice and/or issue a Stage 2 IEP: otherwise continue at Stage 1 for two more review periods
	How effective has the differentiation been at Stage 1?	Summary information from monitoring by class or subject teacher based on day-to-day response to Stage 1 provision; child and parents' views	a) Continue b) Modify targets c) Modify strategies d) Issue a Stage 2 IEP
Stage 2 IEP Design	What 'different or extra' provision from that of Stage 1 does the child need?	Examples of pupil's response to tasks at Stage 1	Review of provision at Stage 1 to check that there is a need for 'different or extra provision'
	What are the new agreed areas of concern for this pupil?	Review of information gathered so far	Agree targets
	Under what conditions does the pupil learn/ behave most effectively?	Pupil response to existing provision including parental and child's views	Identify and apply strategies
Stage 2 IEP Review	What progress has been made by the pupil?	All summary information gathered so far	Return to Stage 1 if concerns can now be addressed with Stage 1 provision or less. Otherwise continue at Stage 2 with or without new targets and strategies if satisfactory progress has been made. If not design a Stage 3 IEP
Design of Stage 3 IEP	What additional provision or advice does the child or school need?	Examples of pupil's response to Stage 2 provision; information and advice from identified outside agencies	Review provision to ensure that outside agency involvement is needed; if not implement a Stage 2 IEP
	What are the agreed areas of concern for the pupil?	Review of existing information gathered so far plus advice from outside agencies or specialists	Agree targets
	Under what conditions does the pupil learn/ behave most effectively?	Pupil response to existing provision plus the views of the parent, child and outside agency/ specialist	Identify and apply strategies in response to contribution from outside agencies
Stage 3 IEP Review	What progress has been made by the pupil?	All summary information gathered so far	Consider movement to Stage 2 if targets can be met with a Stage 2 IEP. If progress is satisfactory continue with current stage. Otherwise adjust strategies and targets. If progress is still unsatisfactory consult LEA to move to Stage 4

Figure 5

This is a list of possible sources of information needed to answer the questions outlined in Figure 5 for Stages 1–3 of the Code.

Information	Good	Satisfactory	Cause for concern
Records from previous schools			
Regularity of attendance			
National Curriculum attainments			
Standardised test results			
SATs			
Recorded achievements			
Reports on child in school settings			
Observations about the child's behaviour			
Parents' view of child's health and development			
Parent perceptions of the child's response to school			
Parental information concerning factors which may be contributing to the child's difficulty			
Parental view concerning action that the school might take to help the child			
Child's perception of his/her difficulties			
Child's view of how he/she might best be helped in school			
Additional information from outside agencies e.g. Health, Social Services			
PUPIL'S RESPONSE TO STAGE 1 provision			
Information from medical practitioner			
Information from Social Services re: involvement with pupil			
Information from LEA re: education supervision order			
PUPIL'S RESPONSE TO STAGE 2 IEP			
Information from any other agency which is relevant to pupil in school			
PUPIL'S RESPONSE TO STAGE 3 IEP			

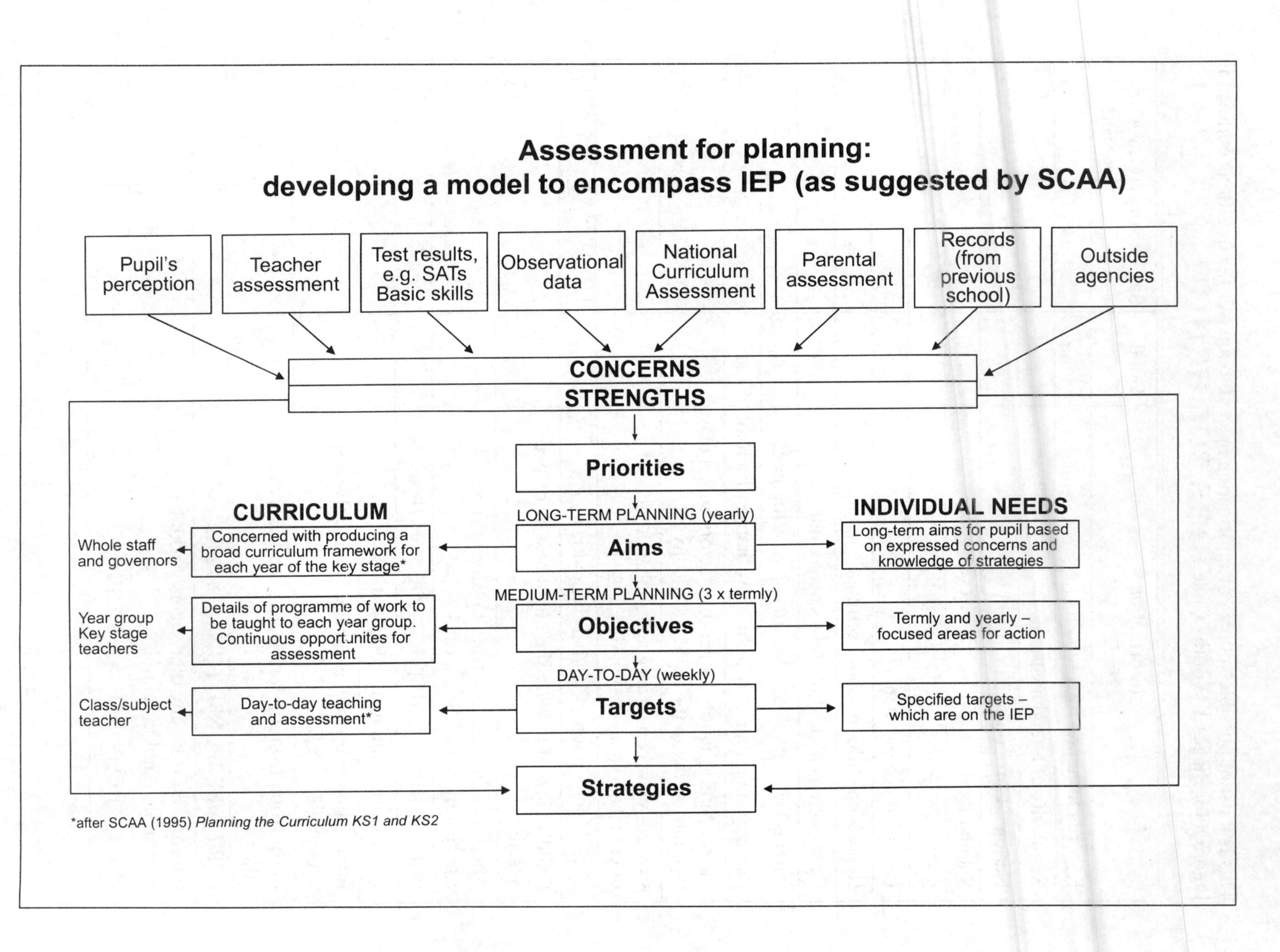
Assessment for planning:
developing a model to encompass IEP (as suggested by SCAA)
Pupil's perception
Teacher assessment
Test results, e.g. SATs Basic skills
Observational data
National Curriculum Assessment
Parental assessment
Records (from previous school)
Outside agencies
CONCERNS
STRENGTHS
Priorities
LONG-TERM PLANNING (yearly)
Aims
MEDIUM-TERM PLANNING (3 x termly)
Objectives
DAY-TO-DAY (weekly)
Targets
Strategies
CURRICULUM
Concerned with producing a broad curriculum framework for each year of the key stage*
Details of programme of work to be taught to each year group. Continuous opportunites for assessment
Day-to-day teaching and assessment*
Whole staff and governors
Year group Key stage teachers
Class/subject teacher
INDIVIDUAL NEEDS
Long-term aims for pupil based on expressed concerns and knowledge of strategies
Termly and yearly – focused areas for action
Specified targets – which are on the IEP
*after SCAA (1995) Planning the Curriculum KS1 and KS2

OHP 3

Assessment: Ideas for action

- Try to ensure that the school's assessment procedures support those needed for the Code of Practice. This can be achieved by examining the school's existing assessment procedures and establishing what needs to be modified or added to support the Code. For example all schools are required to carry out regular assessments of pupil progress, (see OHP 3) including their response to national tests, and report the results to parents. Most schools in addition seek the views of parents either by interview or by school entry questionnaire. Some schools leave a space on record cards to enter information supplied by outside agencies. Assessment for the Code at Stage 1 only requires one additional source of information and that is the 'view of the pupil'.
- Ensure that all those concerned with pupil assessment for the Code are clear about the purpose of assessment.
- Reporting needs to be concise i.e. a *summary* of the information as it relates to the *purpose* of the assessment.

Elizabeth Falconer Hall (1992) suggests that diagnostic assessment underpins effective differentiation to '... find out pupil's experiences, knowledge, understanding, skills and attitudes so that we can plan for the match between curriculum and pupils'.

Methods employed range from the simple and quick to the complex and time-consuming and will depend upon pupils' needs, time allocated and other resources and include:

Unfocused observations	From their experience with a class or pupil, teachers can often locate difficulties that pupils are having in their learning. Whether they are on task, distracted or distracting, seek constant clarification from a neighbour, are able to take turns, or need extra encouragement or explanation to undertake tasks.
Focused observations	As a teacher becomes more aware of the difficulties that a child faces, she can refine her understanding of the problem and attempt some form of intervention. For some behavioural difficulties it may be possible to record its occurrence and frequency so that its triggers and function may be identified.
Checklists and aides-mémoire	These are based upon task analysis of learning areas and will usually be curriculum based. This would include the IEP.
Diagnostic tests	These are often commercially produced tests which may be linked to curriculum modules and may help pinpoint strengths and weaknesses in learning as an aid to future teaching.

Targets: Principles

... central to the notion of IEP planning is the principle of setting learning outcomes in advance as targets to be attained within set time periods (written as what is to be learned not how to increase the learning opportunities).

SENJIT Schools Policy Pack (NCB 1995)

Purpose of targets

To:

- provide a focus for *coordinated educational effort* because everyone involved shares a common goal.
- strengthen the links between policy, planning and provision.
- provide a means for assessing the effectiveness of provision.
- support staff development in relation to SEN.
- provide realistic challenges.
- provide more rigorous criteria for the reporting of progress.
- establish agreed priorities of need.

Rationale

Task analysis assumes that

- what is learned can be broken down into its constituent parts.
- these parts can be described as distinct targets.
- these parts can be set out as a linear sequence.
- the final desired learning outcome can be achieved by meeting each sub-target in the sequence.
- methods of teaching can be identified from these targets.

Targets arise from the assessment of pupil progress within the curriculum and their individual profile of strengths and weaknesses. The *educational effectiveness* of targets rests on their design and selection as well as the shared belief of those involved that they are realistic and worthwhile. The setting of targets can provide a focus for the collaborative educational effort and may involve parents and learners in target setting. Furthermore, planning to achieve targets can direct attention to the efficient use of resources and the direct linking of teaching to learning outcomes.

The achievement of targets can be a measure of the effectiveness of IEPs, and therefore, of the school's SEN provision. It is important to remember, however, that targets do not exist independently. Setting them does not in itself achieve anything, neither does it necessarily result in effective teaching.

Possible pitfalls in writing targets

- What has not yet emerged in the literature is the difficulty that most teachers have, whether specialist or not, in getting the children to make any progress with their IEPs after the teachers have written them. If the child does not make progress on their IEP there tends to be an assumption that there is something wrong with the child. For example, if a child has been identified as having a specific learning difficulty with reading and he or she fails to make progress with their IEP, the assumption is that the child has a more widespread learning difficulty. (MacNamara and Moreton 1997)
- They can lead to a narrow focus for intervention which does not link access and entitlement to the National Curriculum. Critics such as Goddard (1998) consider it to be 'reductionist' and not relevant to any special needs provision.
- They could lead to a false picture of 'effectiveness', i.e. many narrow targets achieved over a short period of time may not be synonymous with real educational progress.
- They could lead to the assumption that *all* learning outcomes can be broken down into small steps. By focusing solely on these steps one could lose sight of the overall outcome and might then believe that the steps themselves, when achieved, *are* the outcome.
- There is a danger that available resources, rather than needs, may dictate targets.
- They may be used manipulatively e.g. if a school feels that a pupil needs additional resources then targets could be selected to evidence 'slow' progress. Alternatively 'progress' could be falsely speeded up by the selection of targets which are relatively easy for the pupil to achieve.
- The achievement of targets might become the *only* indicator of educational progress.
- Targets might become linked to SEN categories e.g. targets for students with Specific Learning Difficulties, targets for students with Emotional and Behavioural Difficulties etc. which assume group homogeneity and the sharing of need/deficit. Published schemes are adopting this approach.

Currently there is an emphasis on SMART (*S*pecific, *M*anageable, *A*chievable, *R*elevant and *T*imed) targets (Lloyd and Berthelot 1992) with some LEAs prescribing that targets must fit these criteria. It should be stressed that this emphasis has sometimes fostered practice which is at odds with the principles of the Code of Practice in that it has lessened learning opportunities for the child.

Setting learning outcomes in advance as targets can be a sound principle for some aspects of teaching, particularly when the content of what has to be taught is highly structured.

However task analysis cannot and should not be used exclusively:

> Beware of tightly defined training programmes based solely on task analysis …
>
> I took a course in speed reading.
>
> After a few weeks I became quite good at it and was able to read War and Peace in thirty minutes.
>
> It's about Russia.
>
> (Woody Allen)

The current favoured model is to provide teachers with guidance on how to write targets and then to provide them with lists of targets linked to categories of need. This method could be useful as a way of improving teacher competence in planning for SEN teaching, provided the aim is not simply to achieve 'technical competence' so that the IEP procedure can 'be seen to be' operational. The design and selection of educationally relevant targets requires more than technical competence. It requires at the very least a knowledge and understanding of individual differences in learning style. An understanding of the substantive issues surrounding teaching approaches which reduce curriculum complexity by deconstruction, for example task analysis, is also important.

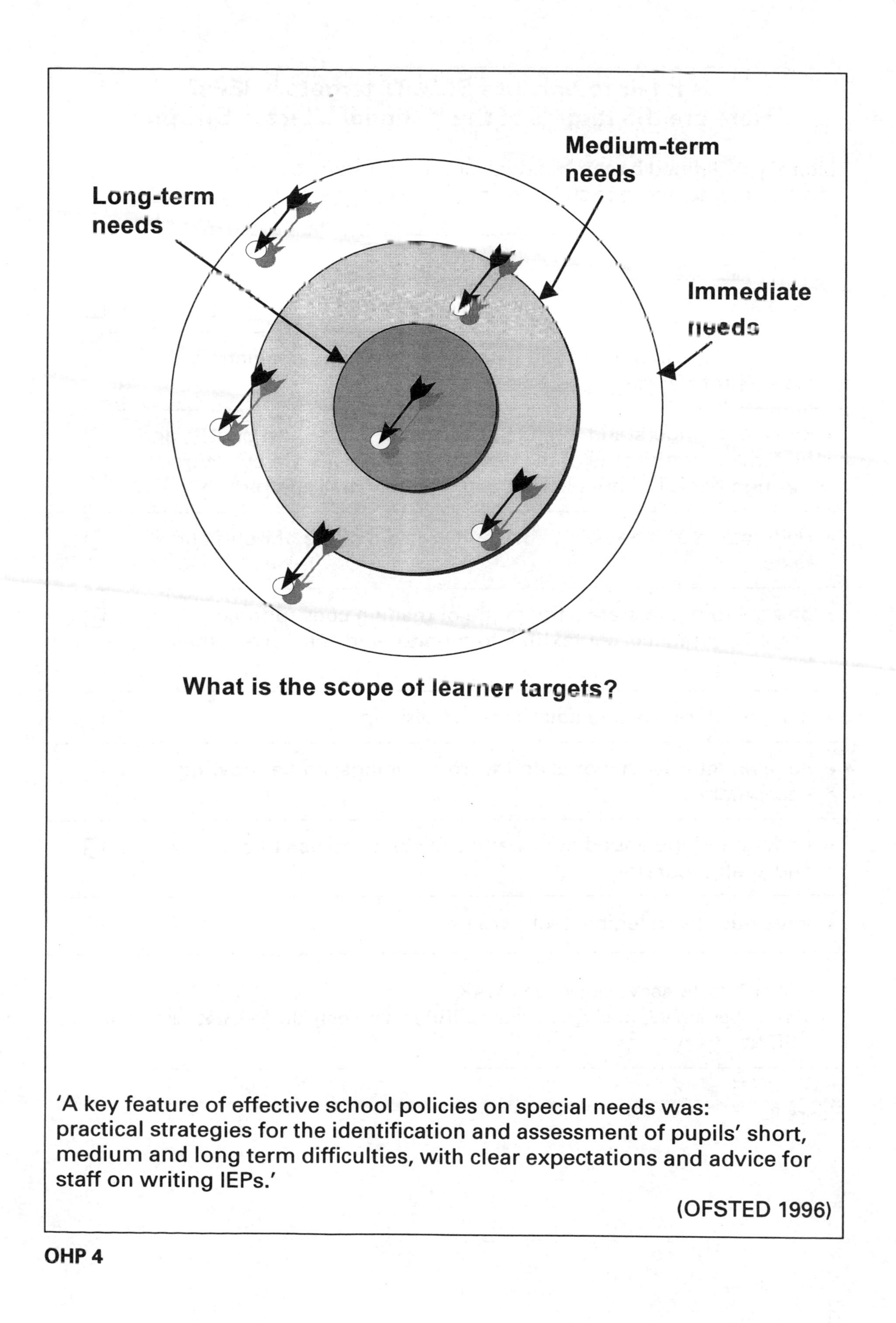
Medium-term
needs
Long-term
needs
Immediate
needs
What is the scope of learner targets?
'A key feature of effective school policies on special needs was:
practical strategies for the identification and assessment of pupils' short, medium and long term difficulties, with clear expectations and advice for staff on writing IEPs.'
(OFSTED 1996)

OHP 4

Is it fair to only use SMART targets in IEPs? Here are the targets of the National Literacy Strategy Literacy is defined by the National Literacy Strategy as, simply, the ability to read and write. Literate children should by the age of 11:	
	SMART?
• read and write with confidence, fluency and understanding.	☐
• be interested in books, read with enjoyment, and evaluate and justify preferences.	☐
• know and understand a range of genres in fiction and poetry, and be familiar with some of the ways that narratives are structured through basic literary ideas of setting, character and plot.	☐
• understand and be able to use and create a range of non-fiction texts.	☐
• be able to orchestrate a full range of reading cues (phonic, graphic, syntactic, contextual) to monitor and self-correct their own reading.	☐
• plan, draft, revise and edit their own writing.	☐
• have an interest in words and word meanings, and a growing vocabulary.	☐
• understand the sound and spelling system and use this to read and spell accurately.	☐
• have fluent and legible handwriting.	☐
• Which of the above targets are SMART? • Is it appropriate for children with an IEP to have only the SMART targets in their IEPs?	

Figure 6

Types of targets

It might be useful to provide teachers with a taxonomy of targets. These could fall under three categories as shown below:

- direct linkage; learning outcome = target
- flexible linkage; target = range of possible learning outcomes
- indirect linkage; target = an outcome which can be recognised but not prescribed

Alternatively targets may be classified as:

- access targets
- process targets
- response targets
- curriculum targets

	Target = direct linkage (learning outcome = target)	**Target = flexible linkage (range of possible learning outcomes)**	**Indirect linkage (outcome can be recognised but not prescribed)**
ACCESS	Will look at teacher when she uses his/her name.	Will make it known to the teacher if he/she does not understand.	Will self-direct his/her attention to the task given to him/her.
PROCESS	Will listen to and repeat instructions given personally to him/her.	Will record information in a notebook when teacher is giving instructions.	Will join in class discussions.
RESPONSE	Will stay on task for period of time set on his/her book.	Will make a brief plan before starting to write and get this checked.	Will respond appropriately to teacher instructions.
CURRICULUM	Will mark six principal cities on a map of England.	Will make maps and plans of a real place.	Will enjoy reading.

In summary

Target setting lies at the heart of the IEP. It requires professional development so that children's learning opportunities are not restricted by a rigid adherence to SMART targets.

> What can be counted might not count.
>
> What counts might not be countable.
>
> (Einstein)

Targets: Institutional self-review

- Do the targets address identified concerns?
- Are targets achievable within a defined timescale for the child?
- Do targets translate into educationally relevant outcomes?
- Do they provide challenges for the pupil?
- Do they create a direct link between planning and provision?
- Do they reduce complexity?
- Do they prioritise aims?
- Are they easily understood by all involved in the IEP?
- To what extent has the design of targets involved all concerned (e.g. pupil and parent)?
- Do targets provide a focus and means for staff development?
- Do they serve to increase the learning opportunity for the child?
- Do targets identify the 'different and extra'?
- Do they avoid isolating and excluding the pupil?

Targets: Ideas for action

Example of Reading aims and targets

This resulted from development work with an LEA learning support team who wanted to provide targets and strategies for primary schools in relation to Reading in the National Curriculum. The result is being used by schools as support material to enable class teachers to become more involved in writing and delivering IEPs.

- **Aim:** to behave like a reader
- **Target:** to look at a book independently for five minutes at a time

- **Aim:** to pretend to read
- **Target:** to join in paired reading with an adult or a peer

- **Aim:** to know how a book works
- **Target:** to look at the text and illustrations when participating in a shared reading activity

- **Aim:** to select an appropriate reading book
- **Target:** to express a preference for the kind of book or a particular book he/she would like to have read to him/her

This is an example how a learner can be taught to act like a reader in a classroom. It does not mean that the child will be able to read. Such are the dangers of applying SMART targets without regard to long-term aims.

A useful exercise for staff would be to compare approaches to target setting for pupils with emotional behavioural difficulties:

Example of SMART targets for Emotional/Behavioural Difficulties

Follow these guidelines in writing behaviour targets for the IEP:

STEP 1: Write down a behaviour which is opposite to and incompatible with the problem behaviour.
e.g. Problem Behaviour = remains apart from other children
Behavioural Target = joins in activities with other children

STEP 2: Use an active verb in the future tense to define the IEP target.
e.g. Behavioural Target = sits at desk/table until asked to move by teacher
IEP target = will sit at desk/table until asked to move by teacher

STEP 3: Work on one behaviour at a time for a term, setting no more than three targets for each problem. Agree the targets with teacher, child and parent.
e.g. Description of problem = he is dependent on teacher
Problem behaviours = i) constantly asks for readily available materials to be given to him before starting work; ii) constantly asks teacher for step by step instructions on how to begin/proceed with written work
IEP targets = i) will take out all appropriate materials on request to start work; ii) when provided with clear instructions, will begin/proceed with written work independently

STEP 4: Set IEP targets according to the hierarchy which you established in your problem profile.

STEP 5: Set targets for the central behaviours from the cluster of behaviours associated with it.
e.g. The cluster of problems = He hits other children, destroys other children's work, shouts out in lessons, refuses to start/complete work, swears at teacher, runs around the class
The central behaviours = runs around the class and refuses to start/complete work (can be described as – out of control and failure to attend to tasks)
IEP targets = i) will sit quietly at the desk throughout lessons; ii) will walk around the classroom (only on request); iii) will start/complete work
(SEN Resource Pack for Schools: McCarthy and Davies 1996)

Behavioural targets may not easily conform to a hierarchy unless *task analysis* is used to break the target down into smaller more achievable steps.

An alternative approach

- Consider the context in which the behaviour occurs. Behaviour serves some function.
- Examine the triggers and consequences.

Factors causing behaviour do not lie within the child all of the time. To frame targets for behaviour effectively, it is necessary to gather facts rather than impressions. Build a picture of when, where and why the behaviour is occurring, using observation sheets if necessary. Gather information about the child's behaviour in different lessons and contexts. Investigate the triggers and responses which might be rewarding the behaviour. Difficult behaviours mainly occur in order to get or avoid something. Look for patterns.

Avoid simple one-liners as explanations of behaviour.

- Look to the long-term needs of the child.
  Does the learner really know what is expected of him/her and if so does he/she have the skills needed to meet these expectations. Social skills might need to be taught?
- If your target is to extinguish a particular behaviour then you must think of an acceptable behaviour to replace it which serves a similar purpose for the learner.
- Set an appropriate target which includes the social and curriculum context in which it has to be achieved.

Target setting in the context of social interaction

The following tables show different mixes of activity and levels of social interaction which need to be considered when planning for teaching and playground activities.

	Alone	Parallel	Group	Interactive
Adult	Child may be colouring – adult initiated.	Adult sits next to child and colours her own picture.	Children are around a table all colouring/painting with adult(s).	Children are working together to produce a coloured picture/ map for display with adult guidance.
Child/ Pupil	Child is doing some maths in his workbook at a desk on his own.	Children are sitting around a table doing their own maths work.	A group of pupils are weighing sweets and putting them into marked packets.	Pupils complete a survey about pocket money and how it is spent so that they can produce descriptive data about their classgroup spending habits.

Dependent ——————————► Independent

Structured	CA sits next to child and reads a book to him while he's playing in the sand.	Child looks at book with adult.	Child reads book to adult – told when to start and finish.	Child reads silently in class when directed.	Child selects a book from school library because he needs it for information to do homework.	Child chooses a book and reads it for pleasure.
Unstructured	Child plays with adult next to him.	Child plays in play-ground with adult supervising.	Child plays alone or watches TV unsupervised in house or classroom.	Child plays next to other children with adult supervision.	Child plays in small group without direct adult supervision.	Child plays co-operatively with other children without direct supervision.

Strategies: Principles

Few teachers use many of them	Many teachers use a few of them

(Hodgon 1995)

How can we work with colleagues to enable the flexibility to select, implement and monitor the strategies that may be needed to meet the targets we have agreed?

The *skill is in making time* to consider how strategies can be applied with an individual learner within the constraints of the classroom and the school.

It may be that only a few strategies are needed for effective learning provided they are consistently applied and monitored.

We have found that some SENCOs regarded a key aspect of the role as that of 'strategy bank' for colleagues, providing 'strategies for all occasions'. However, many teachers have found it difficult to tailor these 'off the shelf' strategies to the identified needs of their child. The SENCO role has developed to support teachers in applying and monitoring strategies as part of ongoing classroom assessment as described by Falconer-Hall 1992.

Many strategy banks for differing learning needs have been developed in response to the Code. Some of those commercially available are listed at the end of this book. They can provide ideas of what may be possible and might work in meeting an individual child's learning needs. Strategy banks have also sometimes become part of the school's differentiation to meet the learning needs of all children through staff development.

However, the sheer number and range of unfamiliar sounding strategies might appear threatening and deskilling to many teachers. In response to this, we attempted to establish the underpinning strategies upon which all the rest were based. We tentatively put forward ten key strategies which underlie the dimensions of differentiation. Individualisation may be based upon these. They are a framework for teachers to consider what they can change in their teaching . We further suggest that this approach addresses the criticism that 'IEPs lead to the creation of deficits within the child'. These strategies focus upon what can be changed within the school to support the next stage of learning for the child.

The 10 Key Strategies(?)

Strategy 1: Clarity of what is expected

less — more

Strategy 2: Predictability/Novelty

less — more

Strategy 3: Affirmation/Criticism (reward system)

less — more

Strategy 4: Interaction/Group Work

less — more

Strategy 5: Available time for tasks (workload)

less — more

Strategy 6: Negotiation/Conflict (choice)

less — more

Strategy 7: Level of work (complexity)

less — more

Strategy 8: Modality

less — more

Strategy 9: Reading demand

less — more

Strategy 10: Attention (given or expected)

less — more

Strategy 1: Clarity of what is expected

Is the implicit etiquette of the school made explicit through verbal and visual explanation? Does the learner know what the task is and how they have to do it? Does the learner know when the task is finished and what they have to do next? Does the learner know the implicit routines of the school and class? Are areas with specific functions clearly marked? Does the learner know 'the way we do things here' and why? Does the child have a personal timetable so they know where they are in the day and during the week?

Strategy 2: Predictability/Novelty

Is the day or lesson structured enough for the child, or is it so structured it is monotonous and boring? Would different activities, groupings and stimuli increase the novelty of the activities? Is enough happening to keep the child involved?

Strategy 3: Affirmation/Criticism (reward system)

Are there opportunities to reward the real effort of an individual? Does the frequency of the reward need to be increased? Are the rewards credible to the learner? Are opportunities for implied or overt negative criticism avoided (e.g. a request for child to perform their weakest skill in front of an unsympathetic audience of peers)? Are social rewards part of the system?

Strategy 4: Interaction/Group Work

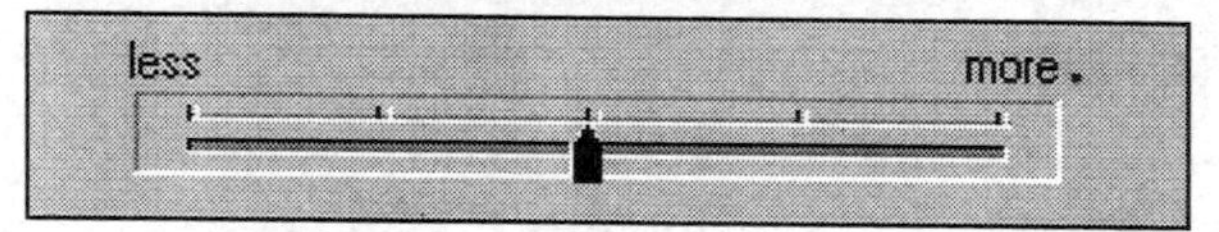

Is there flexible grouping in operation which prevents the negative effect of 'sink' groups? Are learners able to work by themselves if required, or seek appropriate support from others? Are learners encouraged to learn through group discussion and activity?

Strategy 5: Available time for tasks (workload)

Is the workload appropriate for the learner? Has she too much or too little to do? Is the amount of time available for tasks, including homework, enough? Could the learner increase their work rate via the use of a laptop, computer or amanuensis?

Strategy 6: Negotiation/Conflict (choice)

Does the learner have choice? Is she supported to develop independent learning and social skills? Are there opportunities for 'real' negotiation so that serious conflict can be avoided? Is there a flexible and fair system of negotiation available for all learners?

Strategy 7: Level of work (complexity)

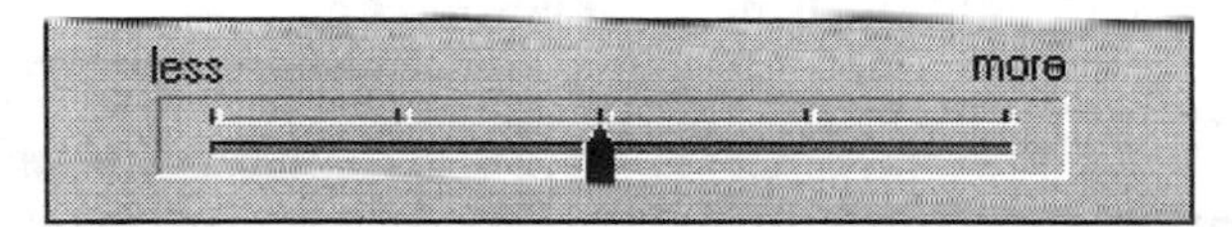

Is the work easy enough for the learner to do? Could it be broken down into smaller constituent tasks? On the other hand, does it set enough challenges? Are links made with other areas?

Strategy 8: Modality

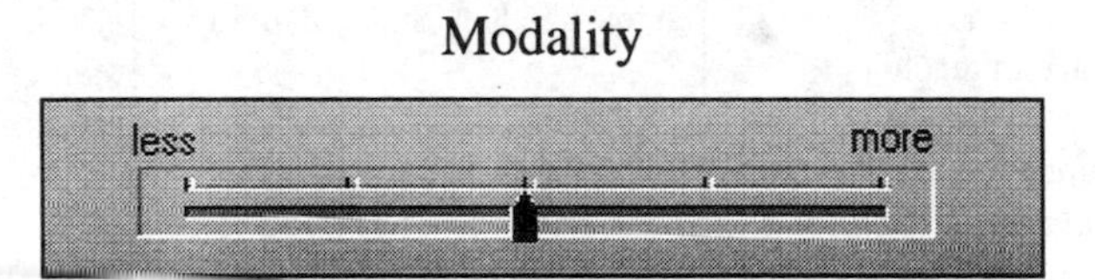

Are tasks set, undertaken and presented just using spoken language? Can sensory approaches be applied so that the preferred modality of the learner is emphasised?

Strategy 9: Reading demand

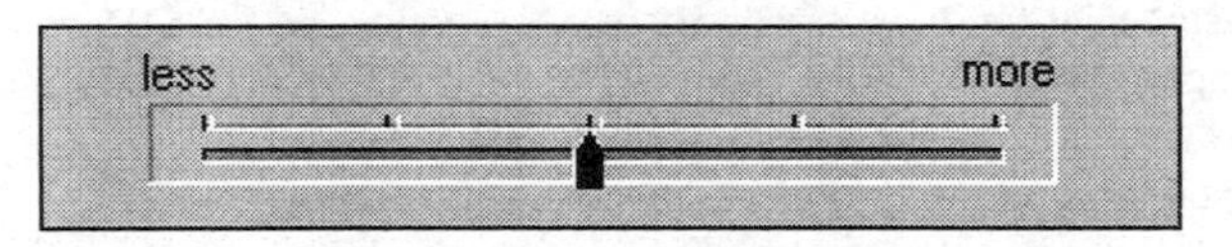

Is the reading demanded from the tasks appropriate? Is the readabilty level too difficult? Is the page layout of materials cluttered or too busy? Do key words need to be taught?

Strategy 10: Attention (given or expected)

Does the child require extra monitoring and support, by the teacher or support staff, in order to keep on task? Can self-help skills and independence be developed?

Strategies: Ideas for action

Most strategies are developments of existing ones that a teacher uses already. The intention of the above approach is to enable the development and application of these strategies more often and more widely. This can be facilitated by planning at different management levels.

The model of planning for differentiation suggested by John Moore (1992) is a good working framework that can help in strategy development.

Planning for differentiation: Stages and dimensions – Implications for management

	Classroom	Key Stage/Department	Whole-school
Curriculum support	Facilitate the development of the twin needs of competence and confidence in teachers to provide a classroom environment conducive to differentiation. Support them in their efforts physically and morally.	Provide a management structure to articulate support and encourage Key Stage planning.	Make clear the responsibilities of the senior management group in providing appropriate management structures and in promoting support.
Units of work	Encourage clear and consistent planning which translates agreed units of work into worthwhile tasks.	Encourage clear and consistent planning which translates programmes of study into worthwhile units of work.	Map cross curricular themes and cross curricular skills and concepts.
Adapting materials	Provide strategies for modifying/adapting materials generated for the unit of work to meet group or individual needs.	Clarify resource policy and planning. Match resource allocation to planned units. Provide time and space to modify/adapt materials.	Develop a comprehensive resource policy.
Groupings	Encourage varied, imaginative and flexible methods of grouping pupils enabling tasks and materials to be allocated appropriately.	Explore the possibilities inherent in 'suiting'. Encourage shared teaching and shared grouping.	Develop a grouping policy. Construct a more enabling timetable.
Support for individuals	Provide strategies for identifying and responding to individual (and in some instances, special) needs.	Ensure consistency of approach. Explore 'internal' support.	Develop policies aimed at consistency of approach. Coordinate responses.
Assessment	Encourage methods of assessment which are curriculum based, and which inform current teaching and future planning.	Ensure consistency of approach. Embed assessment into units of work.	Develop a policy for assessment. Coordinate responses. Ensure continuity.

Monitoring: Principles

For the IEP to work it needs to be monitored to ensure that the plan is being put into practice and is making use of the strategies and resources that have been identified in the IEP. The IEP states what is *different* or *extra* that is needed. This needs to be monitored by those involved. It is an ongoing process, not a retrospective record of failure.

Monitoring arrangements should relate to the information recorded on the IEP documentation. These arrangements are most successful when they are integrated into existing whole-school assessment and monitoring procedures and when the whole school takes on the responsibility.

	The sum of all IEPs	**IEP**
Learner	Not applicable	Is my IEP helping me?
LSA/CA	Am I managing the IEP process for all my pupils? Am I making efficient use of resources?	How effective is my delivery of the IEP? How well is the pupil responding?
Class or subject teacher	Am I managing the IEP process for all my pupils and the staff involved? Am I making efficient use of resources (human and otherwise)?	How effective is the (or my) delivery of the IEP?
SENCO	How effective is the IEP procedure for pupils in this school? How manageable is the IEP procedures in this school? What are the implications for whole-school development?	Does the IEP procedure conform to COP (and LEA) requirements e.g. Does the IEP need to be changed? Are the review dates being adhered to? Is everyone concerned clear about their roles and responsibilities? Has sufficient assessment data been collected to inform the next stage of action?
Outside agencies	How many IEPs is our agency concerned with in the school? Is our involvement with the school's IEPs effective and what are our resource implications?	Is our advice being effectively applied via delivery of the pupil's IEP? Is the pupil making progress as anticipated?
Parents		Is my child making progress? Is he/she receiving the provision agreed on the IEP? Is my contribution valued and effective?
SMT	Is the IEP procedure being effectively managed in the school? Are the pupils making progress? Do the school's IEP procedures conform to the COP and LEA requirements? Are the IEP procedures consistent with the school's SEN policy? Are the pupils receiving the provision described on their IEP? What are the implications for? • school development • budget and resource allocation.	Are individual pupils making progress as expected? Are there any problems with any individual IEPs which may be addressed by the SMT (e.g. parental concerns)? Are strategies cited on individual IEPs consistent with school policy? (This arises in particular with EBD pupils.)

Roles and responsibilities

The IEP can be seen as being supported by a team of all those who are involved. The child and parents are central to this team and should be encouraged to participate as far as they are able. The monitoring process will be carried out by the different members of the IEP team with varying frequencies and for different purposes. The SENCO acts as a facilitator – all information is filtered through the SENCO.

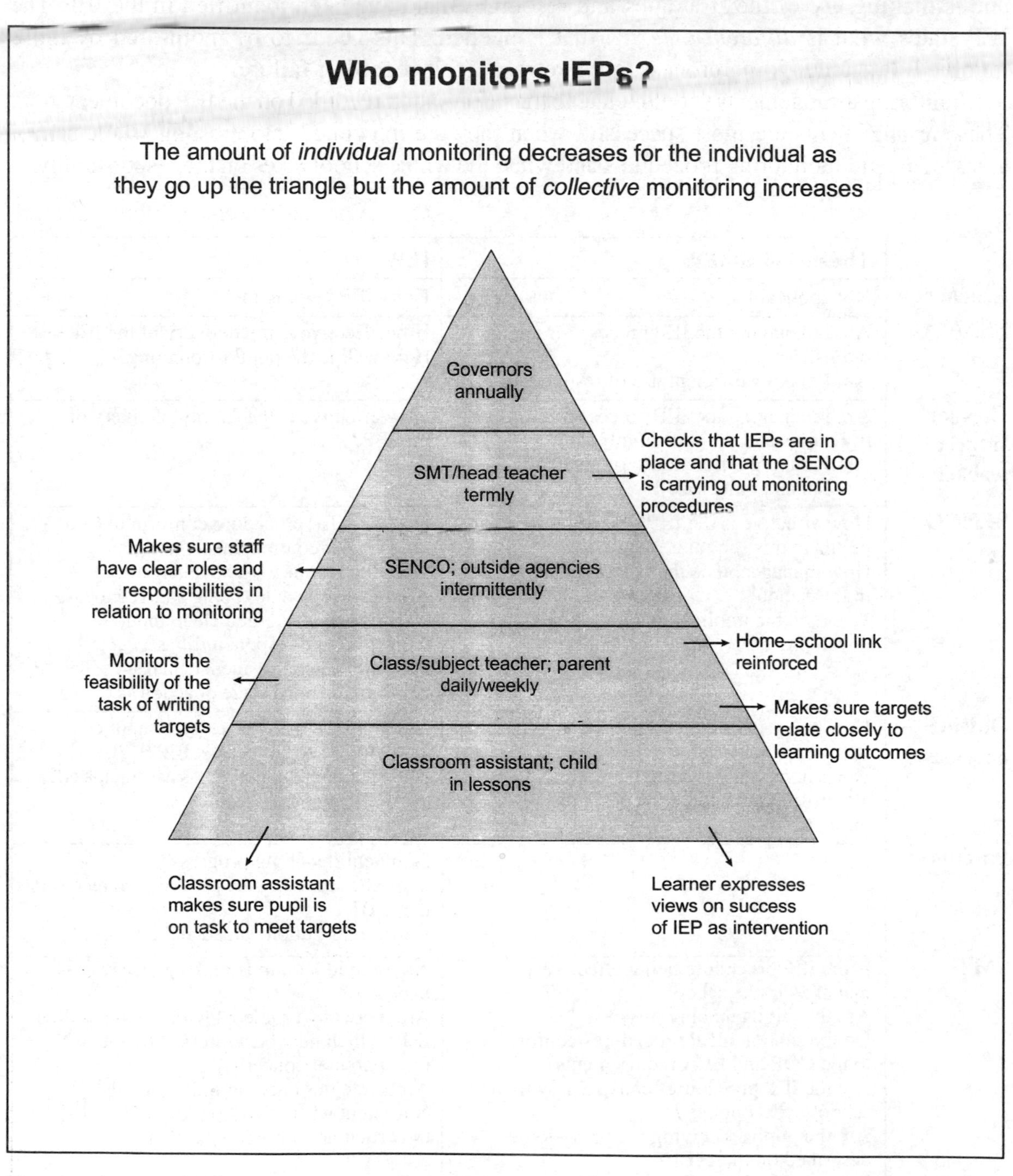

Figure 7

The IEP is a *brief working plan* that may need to be altered as a result of monitoring.

The notion of progress

As noted by McNamara and Moreton (1997), some teachers have found it difficult to monitor progress towards targets.

SCAA suggest:

Progress for pupils with learning difficulties might:

- follow the same pattern for other pupils but take much longer for each stage;
- take place in some areas but not in others;
- take place when pupils transfer things they have learnt in one context to another situation;
- show itself in their responses to stimuli, even if they do not make discernible progress in acquiring knowledge or skills;
- be evident from their reduced needs for support in carrying out particular tasks;
- reveal itself in pupils' ability to demonstrate the same achievement on more than one occasion.

(SCAA 1996)

SCAA further note that the type and degree of response to teaching may be worth noting and sometimes recording. This could form part of the ongoing classroom assessment described by Falconer-Hall 1992. In some cases this might be carried out by an L.S.A.

These responses may include:

- the pupil's use of interesting strategies;
- surprising or unusual reactions;
- breakdowns in understanding;
- what learning took place and where difficulties occurred;
- the degree to which curricular objectives and other targets for each pupil have been achieved.

(SCAA 1996)

How daily monitoring might take place

(A blank proforma is in the Appendix)

PERSON RESPONSIBLE AND PURPOSE OF MONITORING	**General questions asked by the person who delivers the IEP concerning the child's response to his/her IEP**	**Task: Possible Action**	**Strategy resource Possible Action**	**Setting/Context: Possible Action**
Learning Support, Child in Class, Parent. 'Did today's session achieve its learning outcomes? If not what changes may be appropriate?	Is the child interested and on task for most of the session?	Can I make the task more relevant?	Can I get the child more *actively* involved by personalising the task?	Change grouping: would pupil rather work with a peer?
	Is he/she able to understand the task? (i.e. access)	Should I break the task down into smaller steps?	Change mode of presentation from verbal to visual. Reduce the speed of presentation.	Would it be appropriate for me to give the pupil first-hand experience via school visit?
	Is he/she able to process the information?	Is the task linked to something he/she knows already?	Can I get the child to *actively* process material by giving assistance to study skills, and emphasising metacognition?	Would a collaborative small group setting be more appropriate than 1–1 support?
	Is he/she able to give appropriate responses to the task?	Assist with responding in small steps–allow sufficient *time* for a response to be generated. Clarify and highlight key areas of the task to direct child's attention.	Is the required answer simply too difficult i.e. should I 'meet him halfway' by asking for a recognition response before I ask for recall? Or should the correct response be modelled first etc?	Would it help initially if joint or parallel activity was involved to reduce any fear of individual failure?

Figure 8

Monitoring: Institutional self-review

- Do your monitoring procedures enable you to establish the content of the link between the written IEP and classroom practice?
- Does the monitoring inform those concerned about the effectiveness of strategies employed?
- Are all those involved in the IEP process aware of which targets they are working on and how to record progress in relation to those targets?
- Is the working document clear and easy to use?
- Does it tie in with established routines and procedures within the school?
- Is the IEP linked in with planning and assessment at all levels?
- Is time allocated to the monitoring of IEPs?
- Does the monitoring of IEPs result in action? If it doesn't then it is not worth doing.
- Is the monitoring process manageable?

Monitoring: Ideas for action

The following procedures may be used to monitor IEPs:

- class teacher records
- classroom assistant reports
- behaviour contracts
- 'time out' records
- reports from pastoral meetings
- pupil group work records
- departmental 'link' teachers' reports
- home-school books
- in-class support teacher comments
- pupil self-monitoring records
- external specialist reports.

(Warin 1995)

Managing the monitoring of IEPs

Some of the ways in which the monitoring of IEPs is managed in schools are listed below:

One secondary school used a form (see Appendix) which subject teachers and pupils filled in together on a weekly basis. Form tutors monitored these.

In another secondary school subject teachers were asked to indicate progress and areas of concern specific to their subject (see Appendix). They also completed a progress report for the review meeting.

Both of these schools had an SEN administrator as well as a SENCO. In one case the appointment was for half time administration and half time teaching but it remains unclear which part of the post was the more lucrative. In each school the SENCO had designed the information gathering sheet. This may have initially lessened the workload for other staff but it may have created difficulty in the longer term if its purpose and format were not agreed by other staff.

In many primary schools, the learning support assistants played a major role in the monitoring of IEPs. They had day books to record progress which were focused upon IEP targets. The SENCOs met the LSAs on a weekly basis to review progress recorded.

In one school there was a tendency for each Learning Support Assistant to focus particularly on the needs of two of three children with IEPs on a termly basis.

In another primary school the planning and monitoring was done at the same time as midterm planning so that it was part of the whole-school process.

The Scottish experience of implementing IEPs has led to the suggestion of a cyclical planning and review framework termed ASPIRE . This could be used at a whole-school level to assess the entire range of opportunities for learning within a school to meet the targets for an IEP. A diagram of the procedure is shown at OHP 5.

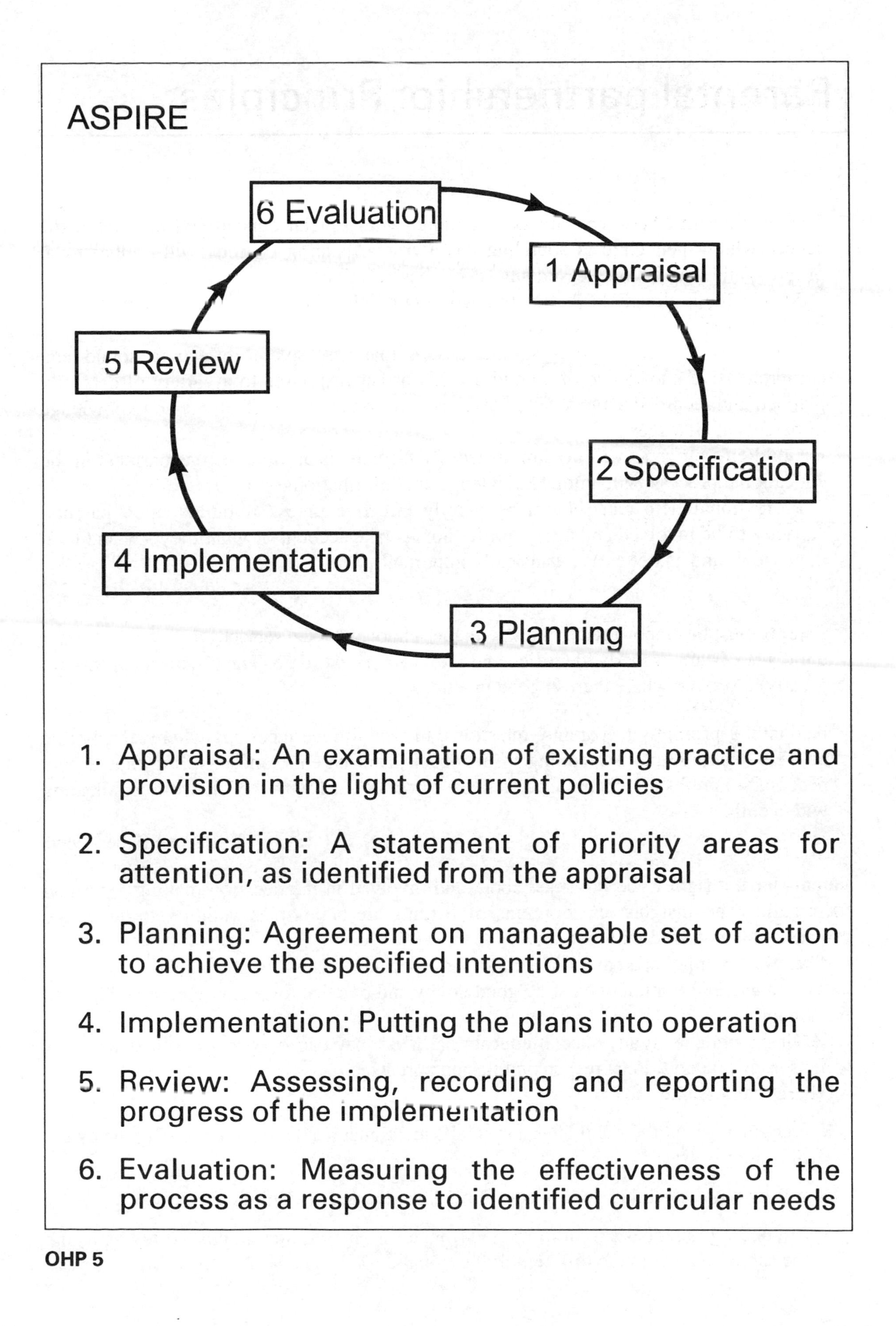
ASPIRE
6 Evaluation
1 Appraisal
5 Review
2 Specification
4 Implementation
3 Planning
1. Appraisal: An examination of existing practice and provision in the light of current policies
2. Specification: A statement of priority areas for attention, as identified from the appraisal
3. Planning: Agreement on manageable set of action to achieve the specified intentions
4. Implementation: Putting the plans into operation
5. Review: Assessing, recording and reporting the progress of the implementation
6. Evaluation: Measuring the effectiveness of the process as a response to identified curricular needs

OHP 5

Parental partnership: Principles

The relationships between parents of children with special educational needs and the school which their child is attending has a crucial bearing on the child's educational progress and the effectiveness of any school based action.

Most schools already have effective working relationships with parents, including the parents of children with special educational needs.

School based arrangements should ensure that assessment reflects a sound and comprehensive knowledge of a child and his or her responses to a variety of carefully planned and recorded actions which take account of the wishes, feelings and knowledge of parents at all stages.

Children's progress will be diminished if their parents are not seen as partners in the educational process with unique knowledge and information to impart.

Professional help can seldom be wholly effective unless it builds upon parents' capacity to be involved and unless professionals take account of what they say and treat their views and anxieties as intrinsically important.

(Code of Practice 2:28)

Parents must be empowered to work with the school and local services to ensure that their child's needs are properly identified and met from the word go. The prospects of this are greatly improved where there is good practice;

responding promptly to parents' questions, in face to face meetings wherever possible actively seeking, and responding to, feedback from parents; and ensuring that, where necessary, parents are encouraged to make direct contact with the LEA officers dealing with a child's case.

(Green Paper 1997)

Parents have a right to be informed about and involved in the decision making regarding their child. The insights and opinions of parents are at least as valid as those of the professionals involved within the IEP.

The relationship that a parent of a child with special needs has with the school will be an extension and elaboration of existing good policy and practice for parental partnership with the school.

Having a child with any special educational need may cause extra stress and worry as well as imposing additional responsibilities on parents.

These may include:

- recognising that their child has a special educational need and investigating the extent of those needs;
- coping with the child's special educational needs when the child is at home;
- responding to requests for information from a variety of professionals – often repeating the same information to different professionals;

- discussing with each other the extent of the child's needs and the provision required;
- being an advocate for the child and dealing with the bureaucracy involved with securing appropriate provision;
- ensuring that the child receives this provision.

Why are some parents reluctant to participate with their child's IEP?

They may feel that they do not have the time or the skills to help their child at home. They may also find it difficult to get into school to attend meetings because of child care problems or working patterns.

Some parents may feel guilty about their child's special educational needs and communication from the school may be interpreted as criticism. They may feel they are being blamed for their child's difficulties and this can lead to resentment towards the school. This in turn may be perceived by the school as lack of interest in the school's efforts or even hostility.

> Parents are most likely to take an active part in school life and their child's development when they have clear information about the school's policies and their child's progress.
> (Green Paper 1997)

The Code emphasises the role of parents as partners. OFSTED (1997) maintains that parents should not only be kept informed but that their views should be incorporated into planning. It follows that parents should be given feedback concerning outcomes of meetings even if they were unable to attend.

> Most schools are conscious that the way they inform parents of their child's progress could be improved and that parental involvement in the review of IEPs is often minimal.
> (OFSTED 1997)

Clearly there is a need for schools to continue to develop their policies and practices for involving parents.

Schools may like to evaluate their policy documents with reference to the following criteria.

Parental partnership: Institutional self-review

Whole-school policy on information to parents

- Does the school's special needs policy avoid unnecessary jargon and explain key terms?
- Does the information and communication from the school convey unintended blame or criticism which might cause resentment?
- Does it outline how special needs are addressed through IEPs at Stages 2 and 3 of the Code?
- Is sufficient information available to parents to enable them to register a concern?
- Do parents know the meaning of the terms 'SENCO' and 'LSA'? Is the role of the SENCO in assessment and decision making processes mapped out in relation to IEPs?
- Is information provided on the support available for children with special educational needs within the LEA?
- Is the information available in the language that the parents speak or are arrangements in place for the translation of this information?
- Is the information in a format accessible to all parents?
- Are booklets and leaflets from relevant specialist services, such as Speech Therapy or Occupational Therapy, made available to parents?
- Are parents made aware of local and national branches of voluntary organisations which may be able to offer support and guidance concerning special needs?
- Are parents aware of LEA and parent advocacy and partnership projects that exist locally?
- Are the parents aware that their child has an IEP and what its purpose is?

Communicating with parents about IEPs

- Do staff listen to and value parent concerns?

- Has the school considered how to overcome barriers to communication which exist? For example, nervous or unsure parents may bring a friend, another parent, a parent governor, or representative from a local organisation along to meetings to ensure that the parent remembers to ask all the questions they want to and register all their concerns.

- Does the school provide alternatives to the usual parent-teacher meeting to discuss ways in which the child can be supported?

- Have staff peer reviewed their communication skills with parents?

- Does the school have a parent support group or actively link in with local parents' support networks?

Whole-school policy on parental participation

- Are the parents encouraged to attend meetings about their child's IEP?

- Does the school have a designated person who is responsible for managing the whole-school policy on parent-teacher partnership?

- Has the school developed methods of enabling parents to attend meetings e.g. transport or some form of crèche facilities?

- Are the concerns and aspirations of the parents intrinsic to IEP planning?

- Do the parents contribute to the setting of targets within an IEP?

- Are parents given guidance on ways in which they can support their child in meeting the agreed targets within an IEP?

- Is there sufficient information on how they might encourage and reward their child's progress towards targets?

- Are they enabled to work on particular targets at home via the provision of resources, training and strategies e.g. parental participation in staff development as appropriate?

Parental partnership: Ideas for action

Despite an initial apprehension some schools have reported a dramatic increase in partnership with parents after they 'bit the bullet' and told parents what the SEN procedures were and where their child was on the register.

Further examples of the responses of different schools

School One: Where there were language barriers, community based organisations were able to provide resources including audio and videotapes.

School Two: A small primary school set up a library of games and other materials that parents could borrow to help their children.

School Three: A secondary school provided a number of curriculum workshops for parents to learn how to support their children's homework in different lessons.

School Four: Provided the DfEE booklet *Special Educational Needs – A guide to parents*, which is freely available in a number of community languages, to parents who had been informed that their children were on the special needs register.

They followed this up with an invitation to come into school to watch with other parents the Coventry LEA video *One in Five*, which is also available in a number of community languages as well as having signed interpretation.

School Five: A large urban secondary school encouraged parents of children with special needs to drop in for coffee before school on their way to work or when they dropped their children off.

School Six: Encouraged parents to share strategies that they found useful in addressing pupils' needs at the IEP meeting which they then suggested to other parents as appropriate.

School Seven: Set up a self-help group for parents of children with special needs on the register of the school which shared concerns but also had input from local voluntary groups and advisory teachers and specialists to discuss concerns, strategies and interventions.

Involving the learner and the peer: Principles

Some learners may not be able to take part in their IEPs to a great extent. Nevertheless maximum participation should be an aim in order to foster independence and self-advocacy.

Involving children in their IEPs is also a good way of embedding IEPs into the system. If children expect to be involved in their IEP, staff will continue to use IEPs.

> The benefits are:
> Practical: children have important and relevant information. Their support is crucial to the effective implementation of any individual education plan.
> Principle: children have a right to be heard. They should be encouraged to participate in decision making about provision to meet their special educational needs.
> (Code of Practice 2:35)

Some children may not know that they have an IEP – they may not understand why they are receiving 'extra or different' provision. Involving children in their learning may be difficult but it is likely to be much more successful than not doing so.

Although not a legal requirement, some schools have Student Learning Plans for all students. While time-consuming in administration, these schools report a dividend in terms of positive student attitude and increased motivation. For these schools, the IEP can be an extension and elaboration of existing practice.

Most schools list 'the fostering of independence' somewhere in their policy documents. The IEP should support the long-term achievement of this endeavour. The learner with an IEP can sometimes become heavily dependent upon an adult, such as a learning support assistant, who may be a constant shadow over the child. This might limit the learner's decision making.

If adults solely design and implement the IEP then the learner is likely to become a passive recipient of something they have little control over.

It is becoming less and less tenable to exclude the child from the very process that is intended to help him, but inclusion may still be the exception rather than the rule. 'Pupils are still seldom involved in the development of their IEPs or in reviews.' (OFSTED 1997)

The role of the peer

McNamara and Moreton 1997 have adopted the principles of peer group support and the joint celebration of individual success which are a feature of weight loss programmes!

They suggest groupings 'where everyone is working towards a target, where everyone has the opportunity to be helper and everyone has the opportunity to be helped'.

A number of schools have developed circle of friends, circle time and circles of inclusion as frameworks for peers to support each other and understand the difficulties that a child might have in making and keeping friends or in just coping (see Appendices).

As inclusive approaches are more widely adopted, the importance of the role of the peer will develop. We noted one primary school which had a target for a child 'to ignore name calling in the playground'. A more effective strategy may have included work with the other children to reduce or remove name calling. It seemed as if the most vulnerable was being expected to do all of the work.

Involving the learner and the peer: Institutional self-review

Does every child:

- know that they have an IEP?
- share ownership of the IEP?
- have access to a copy of their IEP?
- know what their targets are?
- know the reasons for arrangements made to support the IEP?
- get asked about how they can contribute to the IEP?
- get feedback about their progress?
- have this progress presented in a form that is understandable to them?
- take part in the monitoring and review of progress?

Involving the learner and the peer: Ideas for action

- The child can be encouraged to write down their targets in their diary or workbooks.
- The child can and should be involved in the monitoring of his or her progress. In some schools pupils had a pre-printed monitoring form attached to their subject exercise books on which they recorded how well they had done in relation to their targets.
- The child has a set time to discuss their progress with staff in tutorials or PSE.
- Pupils are invited to attend review meetings for at least some of the meeting.
- Pupils propose their targets, how they might meet them and in what ways would they like to be helped.

In addition SCAA further suggest that:

> Schools may want to discuss how they can help pupils to assess their own work through such means as;
>
> - encouraging pupils to reflect upon their learning targets and what they have achieved
> - providing opportunities for individual pupils to review their progress regularly with a member of staff
> - using activities within personal, social and health education to encourage self assessment
> - creating opportunities for all pupils to make choices and participate in self-assessment activities through the use of symbols, pictures, objects, signing and computers or other technology
> - using learning materials of schemes which include integrated self-assessment tasks
> - teaching pupils about the content and purpose of records and helping them to make choices about work, photographs or other evidence to include in their own portfolios.
>
> (SCAA 1996)

The role of outside agencies: Principles

> At Stage 3 the school calls upon specialist support to help the pupil make progress.
>
> (Code of Practice 2:99)

Outside agencies provide specialist advice and input to the IEP. This varies between and within LEAs.

> In some lEAs there is little or no specialist support at Stage 3.
>
> (OFSTED 1997)

> Effective collaboration between LEAs, social services departments and health authorities is essential. Too often the fragmentation of services between different statutory agencies, competition and tight budgets has left parents to take responsibility for coordinating provision for their child.
>
> (Green Paper 1997)

When and where they do operate, outside agencies should provide schools with written information on how their different services can contribute to the IEP. Each agency may prefer to work with the school in different ways. Some may offer only assessment, whereas others may wish to work directly with the child. While some services are rigidly fixed, other services may be responsive to negotiation.

OFSTED acknowledges that support services are stretched:

> Some schools are able to cultivate extensive links with external support services which lead to a high degree of external assistance. In some cases this is because those schools are more welcoming (willing to assist with research, accept visitors, join in working party groups, etc) or are more responsive to the LEA's advice and guidance.
>
> (OFSTED 1997)

Outside agencies should try to accommodate the child within his/her own setting.

Until national legislation is in place, schools will have to continue to report evidence of needs arising from IEPs and to press the case for sufficient specialist support.

These points need to be taken into consideration:

- The IEP needs to include information concerning the frequency, nature and timing of the contribution from the external agencies.
- Teachers will require information from the outside agency on how the child's difficulty will impinge on their curriculum learning activities and what differentiation would be appropriate.
- Parents may require accessible information from the outside agency on how the child's difficulty will encroach on the child's learning and how this might affect the family.

Outside agencies include:

- Learning Support Service
- Behaviour Support Service
- Peripatetic Teachers of the hearing or visually impaired
- Educational Psychology Service
- Child Health Services
- Physiotherapists
- Occupational Therapists
- Speech and Language Therapists
- Child and Adolescent Mental Health Services
- Social Services
- Advisory Services for Information Technology to meet SEN
- Educational Welfare Officer

The role of outside agencies: Institutional self-review

- Does the SENCO or school have the local contact for outside agencies?

EWO	☐	SLT	☐	EPS	☐	Occupational Therapy	☐
Physiotherapy	☐	Behavioural Support Service	☐	Social Services	☐	Community Health Services	☐
Learning Support Services	☐						

- Is the SENCO aware of the services that the above provide and how they work locally?
- How effective are the school's arrangement for working with these outside agencies?
- What information does the school have about these services?
- How are all staff made aware of the contribution from external agencies to a child's IEP at Stage 3?
- Does the school have contacts with relevant local voluntary organisations (for example, parents' groups or local branches of national disability groups)?
- What is the role of the LEA in supporting links with these organisations?
- How can the school improve the efficiency of its work with outside agencies?

The role of outside agencies: Ideas for action

When should they become involved ?

Normally the decision to use external support will follow a Stage 2 review. However, strategic early intervention is a guiding principle of the Code and so it says that it may be necessary on occasions 'following discussions about an initial concern between the SENCO, teachers and parents' and after the SENCO has consulted the head teacher and 'considers that early intensive action with external support is immediately necessary'. This will occur infrequently and will usually be because:

- Stage 2 procedures and resources are perceived by the head teacher, SENCO and outside agency to be inadequate in meeting the child's immediate needs;
- failure to involve the outside agency would be detrimental to the child's education or that of his or her peers;
- failure to involve the outside agency would be detrimental to the child's health or safety.

Advice for coordinating outside agency input

- Clarify the level of joint work necessary and possible with each outside body at the commencement of the liaison. Agree definitions of terms.
- Construct a flexible written document with outside agencies which sets out general roles and, more specifically, who is going to do what, and when and where they are going to do it.
- Discuss time management with outside bodies and approach it imaginatively. Just because support has always been offered on a daily or weekly basis doesn't mean it can't be changed.
- Pay meticulous attention to detail when engaged in liaison discussions with outside bodies; prepare well and develop your chairing skills.
- Invest time in negotiating with outside bodies, so that reports and records can be *user-friendly* and, where possible, shared between professionals.
- Active management support is necessary if SENCOs are to fulfil their liaison function. There needs to be an investment of time and resources in setting up liaison systems and relationships.

(Lacey 1995)

Making use of IT with IEPs and administration: Principles

> The Code of Practice encourages those involved in IEPs to explore the benefits of IT to meet the needs of the learner and then secure access to appropriate IT and train all those who are going to be involved in its use.
>
> (DfEE SENCO Guide 1997)

This means that:

- The SENCO must be aware of the potential of IT for different special educational needs.
- The IT coordinator should also have this awareness.
- The classroom assistant needs to be trained in how the software or device can be used.
- The class teacher needs to be informed how the software or device can be used to support curriculum access.

IEPs can have IT built into them in the following ways:

- The use of appropriate and flexible software already available in the school. For example, the learner is encouraged to make use of a word processor to present work.
- Targeting existing software or IT for use by the learner for a specific activity. For example, the learner is encouraged to use a painting program in Art in order to carry out a painting task because of her hand coordination difficulties. Much software in schools is flexible and underused. It may be that software which is employed generally in the school has features which are able to support the learning needs identified within an IEP.
- Specialist resources are made available from the school's stock to meet some aspects of the learner's needs. For example, the allocation of a laptop or overlay keyboard to support a child with writing difficulties or a talking word processor for a learner who needs to hear what he/she has typed.
- Specialist software or devices are loaned by outside agencies; to support an IEP for example, the loan of equipment not normally available within the school's resource base.
- Specialist software or devices purchased from devolved or external budget and allocated specifically to the learner.

Making use of IT with IEPs and administration: Institutional self-review

For some schools the sheer number of IEPs mean that IT is a potential solution to the problems of paperwork. There is a range of commercial software available to deal with IEPs. A useful document on this topic is available from NCET.

The following questions should help in the selection of a suitable IT system:

- Does the system link in with existing administration systems within the school? If it does then clerical staff may understand how the software will work.
- Does the software work on the machines available to the SENCO in the school?
- Does the software link in with LEA systems?
- Is training available in the use of the software?
- What sort of helplines are available to support the program's use?
- Can the software import and export data to and from existing databases within the school?
- Does the software work in a logical way? If the software is a customised version of an existing commercial database it may have particular ways of working which assume some knowledge of how that particular database works. Is this made clear to the user?
- Does the software support educational as well as administrative functions?
- Can target and strategy banks be built up?
- Does the software provide examples IEPs?
- How easy is it to use?
- Can the format of the IEP be changed to confirm to local, LEA requirements? How flexible is the software in supporting the needs of the IEP team?
- Can letter information be organised and printed out in a variety of formats for different members of the IEP team?
- Can the information that is stored be searched, edited and reorganised easily?

Making use of IT with IEPs and administration: Ideas for action

The following are ideas from different schools:

School One: Allocated a classroom assistant the task of maintaining the SEN database on the computer.

School Two: The SENCO and IT coordinator planned a joint training day for staff to become familiar with software and devices that may be useful within IEPs.

School Three: The SENCO used part of the SEN budget to purchase a number of inexpensive word processors that could be targeted within IEPs for children with writing difficulties.

School Four: The SENCO together with the IT coordinator identified a small number of flexible pieces of software from those generally available within the school which could be configured relatively easily to meet targets within a number of children's IEPs and which could be used by classroom assistants.

An example of how IT can support IEPs

This is a screen display from the Time software which was developed as a result of the DfEE IEP project. This shows an information bank containing descriptions, strategies, targets, resources and World Wide Web sites related to different areas of need which are listed on the left-hand side of the screen. This information can be searched, selected and then copied into IEP databases or word processors using the buttons at the bottom of the screen.

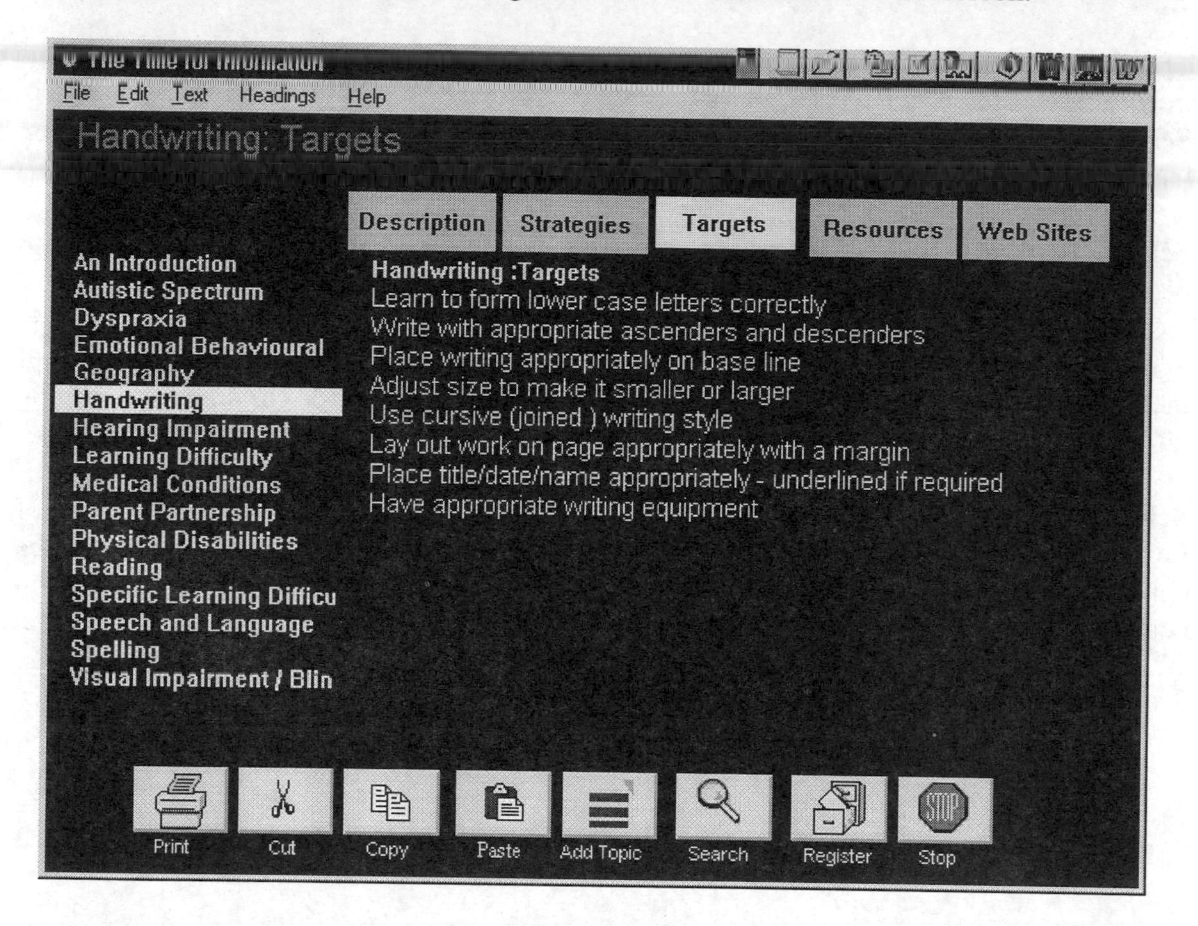

The illustration below shows another screen from the Time software in which previously stored IEP information can be ordered and printed according to different needs. For example, each LSA could be given a list of targets, strategies and resources for each child they supported. The IEP information for each child can be listed by clicking on the right-hand check box. IEPs can be ordered or grouped according to the class teacher or tutor, the strategy employed, the resource, the review date, the concern, the outside agency involved etc. These are listed on the left-hand side of the screen for selection. Summary information about the SEN register or an individual child can also be obtained quite simply by clicking on the appropriate buttons.

Such an IT system can enable a school to think and operate strategically about the individual special educational needs of its pupils.

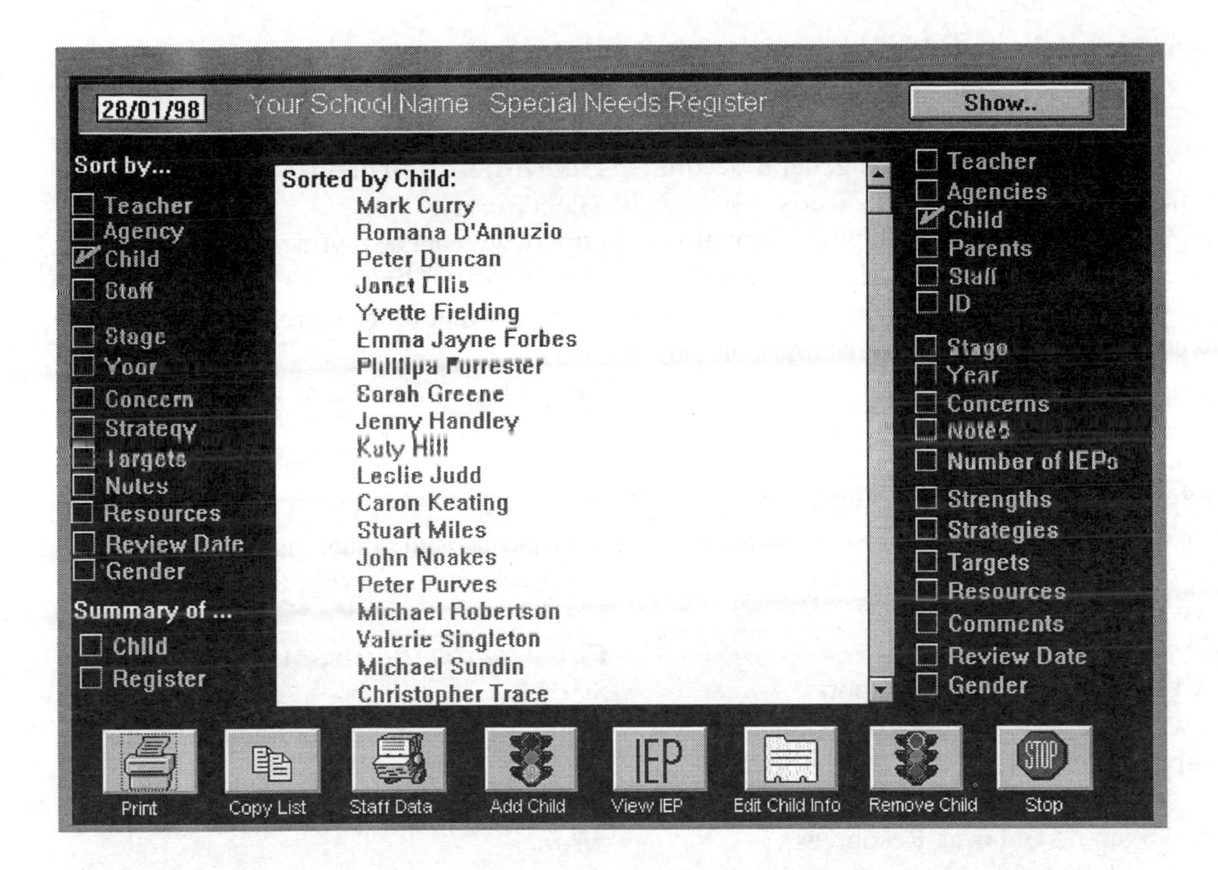

For more information about the availability of the TIME software contact Mike Blamires at the Special Needs Research and Development Centre, Department of Education, Canterbury Christ Church College.

Sources of useful information on the Internet

We recommend that a good general starting point would be the Special Needs Xplanatory, where we will put information related to IEPs and this series of books.

www.canterbury.ac.uk/xplanatory/xplan.htm

Autistic spectrum: web sites
National Autistic Society
http://www.oneworld.org/autism_uk

TheAutism Society of America
www.autism-society.org

All Lewisham Autism Support
www.lewisham.gov.uk/volorgs/alas
very good uk site

Asperger's Syndrome Resources
www.udel.edu/bkirby/asperger/

Carole Grey's social language teaching resources
www.autism.org/social.html

A useful American list
http://web.syr.edu/~jmwobus/autism

Dyspraxia: web sites
The Dyspraxia Foundation
www.emmbrook.demon.co.uk/dysprax/home page.htm

Emotional behavioural: web sites
Attention Deficit Disorder Archive
http://www.seas.upenn.edu/~mengwong/add/

The Mentors In Schools Project
http://www.pncl.co.uk/~prospero/misnet.html

Hearing impairment: web sites
SilentWorlds:
http://www.cant.ac.uk/title/SW/sw_home.htm
A useful set of links maintained by Wayne Barry at Canterbury Christ Church College

Learning difficulties: web sites
Down's Syndrome
http://www.nas.com:80/downsyn/

Viewpoint Home Page
http://www.mencap.org.uk/viewpoint/

Physical disabilities: web sites
SCOPE
http://www.futurenet.co.uk/charity/scope/

Specific learning difficulties: web sites
British Dyslexia Association
www.bda-dyslexia.org.uk/

The Dyslexia Archive at the University of Kent at Canterbury
http://www.hensa.ac.uk/dyslexia.html

Iansyst's Site
http://www.dyslexic.com/
A UK vendor with useful information

Visual impairment/blindness: web sites
Royal National Institute for the Blind
http://www.rnib.org.uk

References

Carpenter, B. (1996) 'The Interface between the Curriculum and the Code', *British Journal of Special Education* **23**(1), 18–20.

CEC (1994) '12 Principles for Successful Inclusive Schools', *CEC Today Newsletter*: May, 13–17.

Cowne, E. (1996) *The SENCO Handbook*. London: David Fulton Publishers.

Cowne, E. (1997) *Presentation at DfEE IEP Conference* unpub: Chichester Institute of Education.

DfE (1994) *Special Educational Needs: A Guide for Parents*. London: HMSO.

DfEE (1994) *Code of Practice on the Identification and Assessment of Special Educational Needs*. London: HMSO. (EDUC JO22465NJ 5/94)

DfEE (1997a) *Excellence for all children: Meeting Special Educational Needs*. London: HMSO.

DfEE (1997b) *Improving Literacy in Primary Schools*. www.open.gov.uk/dfee/seu/literacy/ index.htm

Dwyfor Davies, J. (1996) 'Pupils' views on special educational needs practice', *Support for Learning* **11**(4), 157–61.

Dyer, C. (1995) 'The Code of Practice through LEA eyes', *British Journal of Special Education* **22**(2), 48–51.

Dyson, A. (1997) 'Social and educational disadvantage: reconnecting special needs education', *British Journal of Special Education* **24**(4), 152–7.

Einstein, A. (1996) in Calaprice, A. (ed.) *The Quotable Einstein*. Princeton, NJ: Princeton Univ. Press.

Falconer-Hall, E. (1992) 'Assessment for Differentiation', *British Journal of Special Education* **22**(3), 20–3.

Frier, B. J. and McCormack, A. E. (1996) *Individualised Educational Programmes: Approaches to Design and Implementation: A Staff Development Resource for Teachers*. Edinburgh: Scottish Office for Education and Industry.

Frostig, M. and Marlow, P. (1973) *Learning Problems in the Classroom*. Grune and Stratton: New York.

Garner, P. (1995) 'Sense or Nonsense in the Code of Practice', *Support for Learning* **10**(1), 3–7.

Goddard, A. (1997) 'The role of individual education plans/programmes in special education: A critique', *Support for Learning* **12** (4), 170–3.

Greenhalgh, P. (1996) 'Behaviour: Roles, responsibilties and referrals in the shadow of the Code of Practice', *Support for Learning* **11**(1), 17–24.

Haddow, W. H. (1931) *Report on the Consultative Committee on Primary Education*. London: HMSO.

Hammond, C. and Read, G. (1992) 'Individual v. Individualised: into the 1990's' in Bovair, K., Carpenter, B. and Upton, G. (eds) *Special Curricular Needs*, 135–45. London: David Fulton Publishers.

Hodgdon, L. A. (1995) *Visual Strategies for Improving Communication Vol. 1*: Quirk Roberts Publishing.

Hornby, G. (1995) 'The Code of Practice – Boon or Burden?', *British Journal of Special Education* **22**(3), 116–20.

Keefe, C. H. (1996) *Label Free Learning: Supporting Learners with Disabilities*. London: Paul Chapman.

Lloyd, S. R. and Berthelot, C. (1992) *Self-Empowerment: How to get what you want from life*. London: Kogan Page.

Loxley, A. and Bines, H. (1995) 'Implementing the Code of Practice: Professional Responses', *British Journal of Special Education* **22**(3), 185–9.

Lynch E. C. and Beare, P. L. (1990) 'The quality of IEP Objectives and their Relevance to Instruction for Students with Mental Retardation and Behavioural Disorders', *Remedial & Special Education* **11**, 48–55.

McCarthy, D. and Davies, J. (1996) *SEN Resource Pack for Schools*. Ilford: Specialist Matters.

McNamara, S. and Moreton, G. (1997) *Understanding Differentiation*. London: David Fulton Publishers.

Moore, J. (1992) 'Good Planning is the Key', *British Journal of Special Education* **19**(1) 16–19.

Morgan, D. P. and Hode, C. (1983) 'Teachers' attitudes towards IEPs: A two year follow up', *Exceptional Children* 50, 64–7.

Norwich, B. (1996) 'Special Needs Education or education for all: connective specialisation and ideological impurity', *British Journal of Special Education* **23**(3), 100–3.

OFSTED (1996) *The Implementation of the Code of Practice for pupils with special educational needs*. London: HMSO.

OFSTED (1997) *The SEN Code of Practice: Two Years On*. London: HMSO.

Pugach, M. C. (1982) 'Regular Classroom teacher involvement in the development and utilisation of IEPs', *Exceptional Children* 48, 371–4.

Rankin, P. and Rees-Davies, N. (1996) 'The Code of Practice: In Practice', *British Journal of Special Education* **23**(3), 110–14.

Rodger, S. (1995) 'Individual Education Plans Revisited: A Review of the Literature', *International Journal of Disability, Development and Education* **42**(3), 221–39.

SCAA (1996) *Assessment, recording and accreditation of achievement for pupils with learning difficulties*. London: SCAA. (Publications Ref: COM/96/551)

Schenck, S. J. (1980) 'The diagnostic/instruction link in individualized education programs', *Journal of Special Education* **14**(2), 337–45.

Sinason, V. (1992) *Mental Handicap and the Human Condition: new approaches from the Tavistock Clinic*. London: Free Association Books.

Smith, S. (1990) 'Comparison of Individualized Learning Programs (IEPs) of students with Behavioural Disorders and Learning Difficulties' *The Journal of Special Education* **24**, 85–99.

Smith, S. W. (1990) 'Individual Education Programs (IEPs) in special education – from intent to acquiescence', *Exceptional Children* 56, 6–14.

Thomas, G., Walker, D., Webb, J. (1997) *The Making of the Inclusive School*. London: Routledge.

Tod, J. (1996) *Special Educational Needs: The Working of the Code of Practice and the Tribunal*. Education Committee Second Report, p. 34. London: HMSO.

Warin, S. (1995a) *Implementing the Code of Practice – Individual Education Plans*. Stafford: NASEN.

Warin, S. (1995b) 'Individual Extreme Panic (IEP)' *Special!* Autumn, 19–23.

Warnock, H. M. (1978) *Special Educational Needs*. London: HMSO.

Webster, A. and Cane, F. (1995) 'IEPs Teaching and Learning', *Special Children* September, 1–12.

Wedell, K. (1995) 'Making Inclusive Education Ordinary', *British Journal of Special Education* **22**(3), 100–4.

Other resources

The NC programmes of study in Small Steps
B. Byrom
24 Millview Gardens
Shirley
Croydon CR0 5HW
Tel. 0181 565 0040

One In 5 (video)
A parent's guide to special educational needs
Public Relations Unit
The City Council, Coventry
Tel: 01203 833 333

NCET web pages
http://www.ncet.org.uk/senco/legislation/sencode.htm/#computer
Making use of IT in IEPs.

SENJIT (1995) *Schools' SEN Policies Pack*. London: National Children's Bureau.

Appendices

	Page
Do you recognise your school's IEPs?	82
IEP summary	83
Targeting needs with an IEP	84
Examples of IEP proformas	85–95
Secondary schools: subject-based IEPs?	96–98
A completed IEP	99–101
Obtaining non-verbal responses	102
Daily monitoring proforma	103
Resources for peer support	104

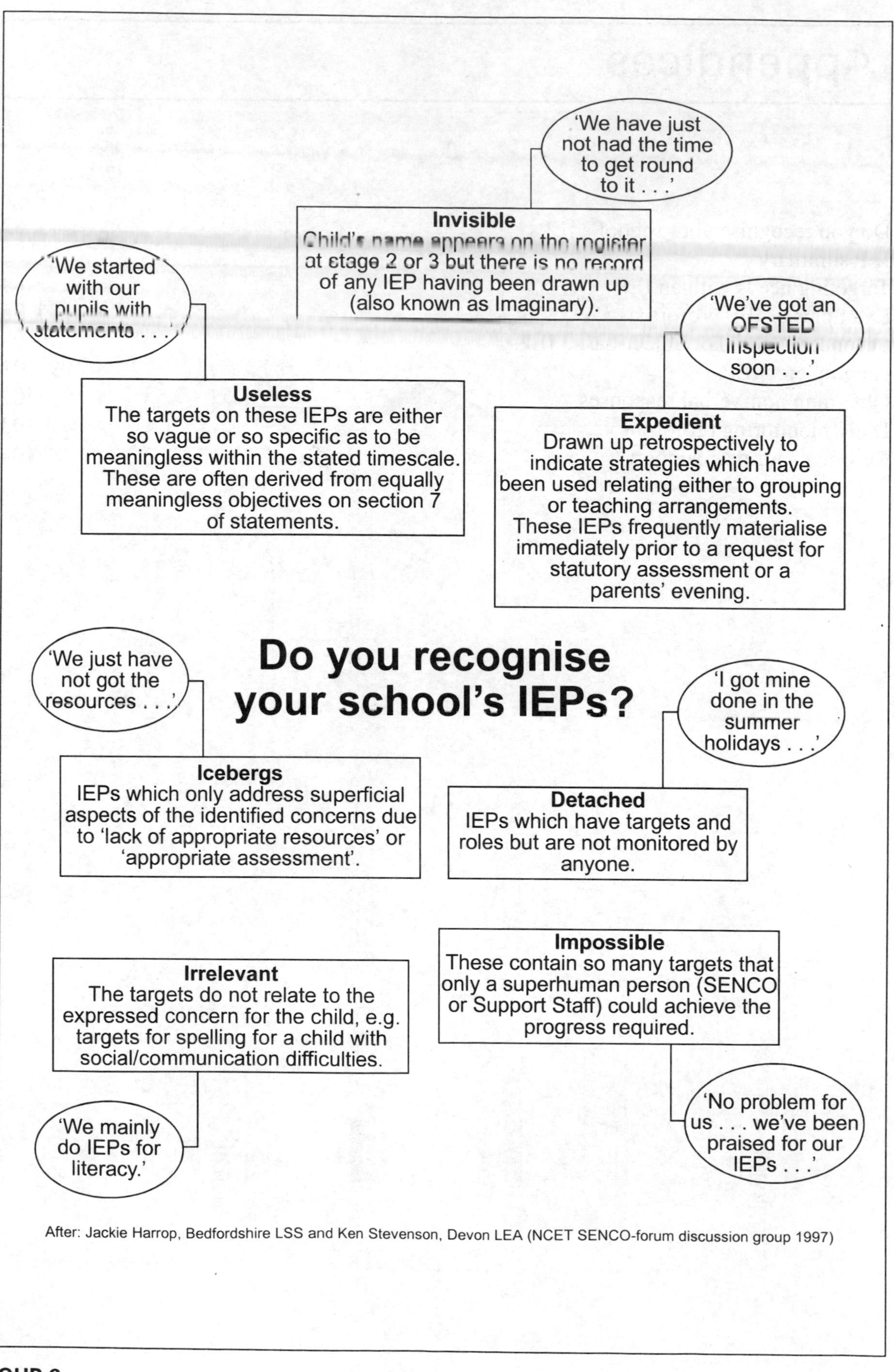
'We have just not had the time to get round to it . . .'
Invisible
Child's name appears on the register at stage 2 or 3 but there is no record of any IEP having been drawn up (also known as Imaginary).
'We started with our pupils with statements . . .'
Useless
The targets on these IEPs are either so vague or so specific as to be meaningless within the stated timescale. These are often derived from equally meaningless objectives on section 7 of statements.
'We've got an OFSTED inspection soon . . .'
Expedient
Drawn up retrospectively to indicate strategies which have been used relating either to grouping or teaching arrangements. These IEPs frequently materialise immediately prior to a request for statutory assessment or a parents' evening.
Do you recognise your school's IEPs?
'We just have not got the resources . . .'
Icebergs
IEPs which only address superficial aspects of the identified concerns due to 'lack of appropriate resources' or 'appropriate assessment'.
'I got mine done in the summer holidays . . .'
Detached
IEPs which have targets and roles but are not monitored by anyone.
Impossible
These contain so many targets that only a superhuman person (SENCO or Support Staff) could achieve the progress required.
Irrelevant
The targets do not relate to the expressed concern for the child, e.g. targets for spelling for a child with social/communication difficulties.
'No problem for us . . . we've been praised for our IEPs . . .'
'We mainly do IEPs for literacy.'
After: Jackie Harrop, Bedfordshire LSS and Ken Stevenson, Devon LEA (NCET SENCO-forum discussion group 1997)

OHP 6

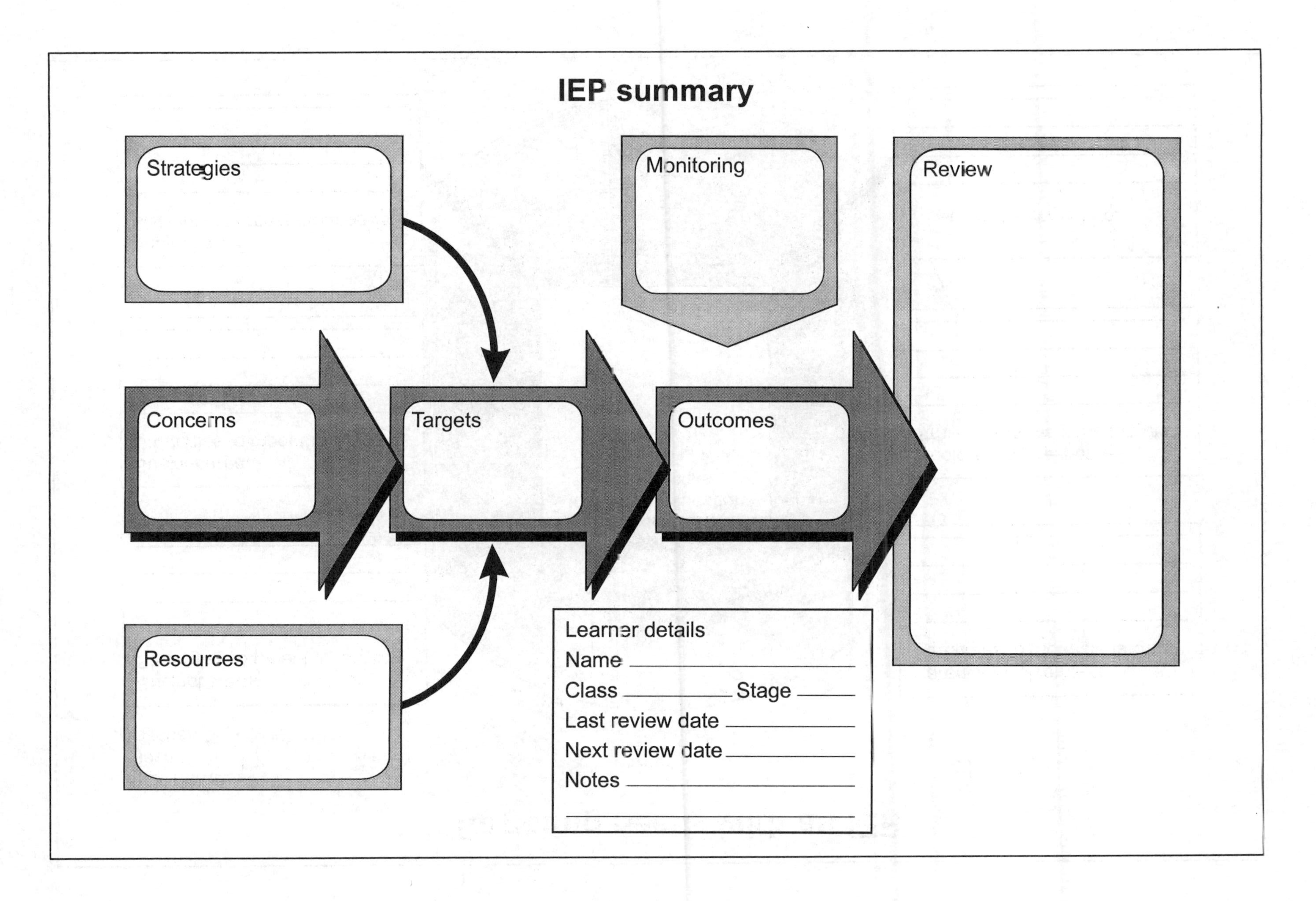
IEP summary
Strategies
Monitoring
Review
Concerns
Targets
Outcomes
Resources
Learner details
Name
Class
Stage
Last review date
Next review date
Notes

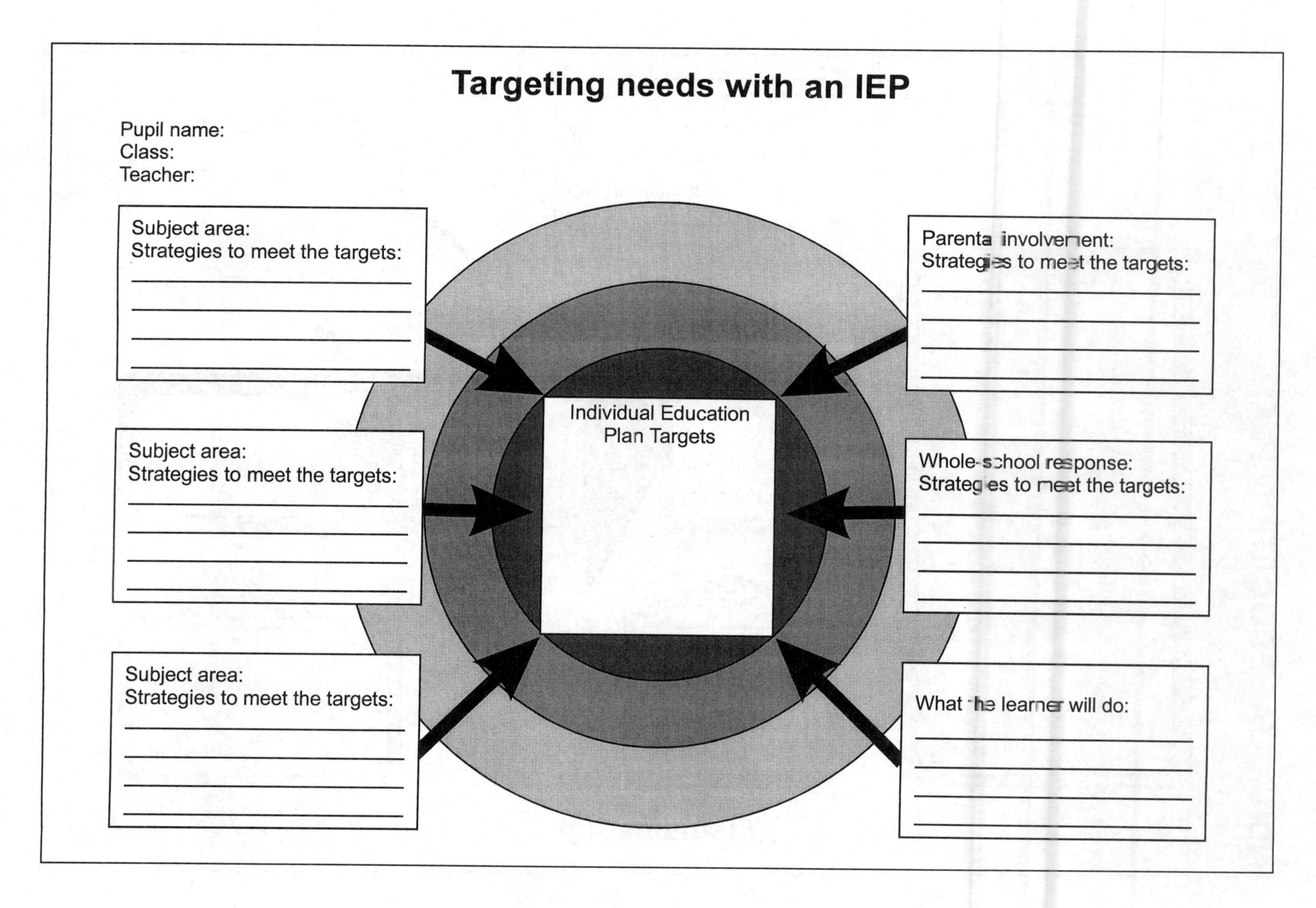
Targeting needs with an IEP
Pupil name:
Class:
Teacher:
Subject area:
Strategies to meet the targets:
Subject area:
Strategies to meet the targets:
Subject area:
Strategies to meet the targets:
Individual Education
Plan Targets
Parental involvement:
Strategies to meet the targets:
Whole-school response:
Strategies to meet the targets:
What the learner will do:

INDIVIDUAL EDUCATION PLAN

Name:	Date of Birth:
Date:	Form:
Description of Abilities:	
General Strategies:	
Parental Support:	
Learning Support Strategies:	
External Input:	
Pupil's Targets:	
Personnel Involved:	
Review Date:	

INDIVIDUAL EDUCATION PLAN

CURRICULUM TARGETS
Art Design and Technology
Business and Information Studies
English
Geography
History
Mathematics
Modern Language
Performing Arts
Physical Education
Religious Studies
Science
Sociology

INDIVIDUAL EDUCATIONAL PLAN FOR:			D.O.B
LEARNING DIFFICULTIES	TARGETS SET	PERSONNEL INVOLVED	MEDICAL/PASTORAL REQUIREMENTS
ACTIVITIES, MATERIALS AND EQUIPMENT		PARENTAL CONTRIBUTION	MONITORING/ASSESSMENT ARRANGEMENTS
			REVIEW DATE
			COMPLETED BY DATE

INDIVIDUAL EDUCATION PLAN

Child:	Date:	NCY:	Stage:	Last ISR:

Nature of the Needs:	Provision (frequency and timing) Staff (please colour-code and give ratios)	M			
		T			
	1.	W			
	2.	T			
	3.	F			

External Specialist Support:

Pastoral or Medical Requirements:

Main Targets	Strategies	Outcome
Sub-Targets		

Parental Involvement	Child's View	Other Action Agreed	REVIEW DATE Signed SENCO

INDIVIDUAL EDUCATION PLAN

Pupil's Name:	NC Year and Class:	Date:

Stage 2 ☐ Stage 3 ☐ Statement ☐

AREA(S) OF DIFFICULTY	TICK	COMMENT
Reading		
Spelling		
Handwriting/presentation		
Comprehension of written materials		
Numeracy		
Oral ability		
Following instructions		
Work rate/completion of tasks		
Motivation		
Concentration		
Motor control		
Physical/sensory		
Behaviour		
Cooperation with adults		
Cooperation with peers		
Self-esteem/confidence		
Personal organisation		
Sequencing		
Auditory memory		
Visual memory		

PRIORITY AREA(S)

OUTLINE OF SPECIAL EDUCATIONAL PROVISION

INDIVIDUAL EDUCATION PLAN

Pupil's Name:	NC Year and Class:	Date:

TARGETS

1.

2.

3.

STRATEGIES TO BE EMPLOYED

SUPPORT TO BE PROVIDED

People involved	Frequency and timing	Focus of support
Class teacher/form tutor		
SENCO		
CA		
IPS		
EP		
Parents		
Pupil		

PARTICULAR REQUIREMENTS (Medical, pastoral care, materials or equipment)

INDIVIDUAL EDUCATION PLAN

Pupil's Name:	NC Year and Class:	Date:

MONITORING AND ASSESSMENT ARRANGEMENTS

REVIEW ARRANGEMENTS

Review Date:

ISR Date:

People Involved:

Information Required:

Signed: (SENCO)	Date:
Signed: (Head teacher)	Date:

DISTRIBUTION

Form tutor/Year tutor	☐	Parents	☐
CA	☐	IPS	☐
Subject teachers (specify)	☐	Other (specify)	☐

INDIVIDUAL EDUCATION PLAN

PUPIL INFORMATION

1.

Level of Support

Name: ____________________	DOB: [ ]	YR [ ]	Y1 [ ]	Y2 [ ]	Y3 [ ]
Class/Teacher: ________________	NCY: [ ]	LIB/EIP	LIB/EIP	LIB/EIP	LIB/EIP

INFORMATION GATHERED From class teacher (class records; profiles; reports from within school; observations). From parent (medical and development; progress and behaviour; possible action plans). From pupil (view of performance and how these might be addressed). From other sources (Stage 2 information already available from Health, Social Services, EWS, EPS, IPS, PD/SIS and voluntary organisations); (Stage 3 the doctor or GP on medical advice; Social Services re supervision orders, SSD involvement with the family, concerns about welfare, CPC etc.).

SUMMARY OF FINDINGS

NATURE OF NEED

CONTRIBUTORS: CT HT SENCO

CA Parent/Carer Agencies Date: / /

2.

SPRING TERM	
PRIORITY AREAS IDENTIFIED AS AREAS TO WORK ON	(1) (2) (3)
TERM'S TARGETS	(1) (2) (3)
STRATEGIES	
MATERIALS/EQUIPMENT required	
MEDICAL/PASTORAL arrangements	
PARENTAL CONTRIBUTION	
FREQUENCY AND DURATION OF SUPPORT by school by external agencies	
MONITORING AND ASSESSMENT ARRANGEMENTS including date of review	/ /

3.

SUMMER TERM	AUTUMN TERM
(1) (2) (3)	(1) (2) (3)
(1) (2) (3)	(1) (2) (3)
	/ /

4.

REVIEW FORMS OF INDIVIDUAL EDUCATION PLAN for ____________________

SPRING TERM Date: / /	PERSONNEL: CT SENCO PARENT AGENCIES CA HT PUPIL
Progress made by pupil: (1) (2) (3)	
Updated Information	Pupil Assessment
	Parent Assessment
	Future Action

SUMMER TERM Date: / /	PERSONNEL: CT SENCO PARENT AGENCIES CA HT PUPIL
Progress made by pupil: (1) (2) (3)	
Updated Information	Pupil Assessment
	Parent Assessment
	Future Action

SECONDARY SCHOOLS: SUBJECT-BASED IEPs?

Should secondary schools set *common targets* for IEPs across all subjects?

An example of an IEP which could be used by *all* subject teachers would be:
1.

Name....................................... Form................ SEN Stage.......... Review __/__/__		
TARGETS	for ____________	Subject Teachers requested to
• **Handwriting**	• to be able to write clearly most of the time	• check on and reward (with use of IT room) for good effort and use of penhold • provide practice sheets with subject specific words for current work (5 words per week)
• **Spelling**	• to develop a personalised dictionary with illustrations	• assist with choice of appropriate subject words (2 words per week) • encourage and reward its use
• **Behaviour**	• to control outbursts of frustration	• to allow 'time out' when needed

Another way of dealing with common targets but with different roles assigned might be like this i.e. still only with one piece of paper:

NAME:		DATE: REVIEW DATE:		
Functional Area	Long-term Aims	Targets	Methods and Equipment	Person Responsible
Home and Family				
Physical and Medical				
Educational and Vocational				
Emotional and Behavioural				

Presumably some overlap in targets could occur and a space for *Common Targets* at the top of the sheet might be helpful, although there are 'Pupil Targets' on the previous sheet. The implication is that *subject teachers* will write at least some of the targets.

Guidance for subject teachers in search of a strategy with regard to target setting

The following plan could be used by a secondary SENCO to gather information from subject teachers, thus creating an opportunity for their involvement:

INDIVIDUAL EDUCATION PLAN		
Name	Form	SEN Stage
Subject	Teacher	
IEP Coordinator	Review Date	

TARGETS

How will you support the student working towards these targets?

What targets would you like to be achieved in your subject?

Successful strategies thus collected might be collated to provide a resource for everyone: 3.

TARGET	PRESENT BEHAVIOUR	SUGGESTED ACTION
• To *attempt* all written tasks	• reluctance to produce written work (struggles with literacy skills)	• give sentences or paragraphs to sequence
		• praise *all* attempts
		• encourage use of laptop computer
		• make provision for reorganisation of information i.e. from one form to another, for example: diagram → text; text → flow chart; picture → text/concept map
		• give a glossary of useful words
		• cloze activities or student leaves gaps when unsure, with encouragement to use first letters
		• start the student off by writing 1 or 2 sentences for them

In addition, however, some schools have found that planning for differentiation at the time of undertaking medium-term planning helps in establishing useful strategies.

INDIVIDUAL EDUCATION PLANS

STAGE:

1.

Pupil:	Date of Birth:				National Curriculum Year Group:

Nature of Concern:	Date:

TARGETS to be addressed in a given time	STRATEGIES e.g. programmes, activities, materials, equipment, staff, frequency, parental involvement, pastoral, medical, external specialists	EVALUATION OF TARGETS monitoring and assessment arrangements; involve staff, pupil, parents	REVIEW include date and people involved

2.

INDIVIDUAL EDUCATION PLAN CURRICULUM TARGETS:
Art Design and Technology
Business and Information Studies
English
Geography
History
Mathematics
Modern Languages
Performing Arts
Physical Education
Religious Studies
Science
Sociology

3.

Pupil: Adam Radcliffe **D.O.B:** 17|12|86 **N.C. Year Group:** 6 **School:** G.G.M.S. **Date:** 4.10.95

Nature of Concern: Lack of motivation to write or work in class. Poor spelling age (6.10; Vernon). R.A. 6.8 years. Reading age has slipped back from 7.1 years in January 1995.

TARGETS	ACTION	EVALUATION OF TARGETS	REVIEW
to be addressed in a given time	e.g. programmes, activities, materials, equipment, staff, frequency, parental involvement, pastoral, medical, external specialists	monitoring and assessment arrangements	include date and people involved
To get Adam to the stage where he wants to write and is keen to be withdrawn for support.	Adam and I will write a book about his passion – motorbikes. He will dictate the text to me and I will type it up using Phases 3 with sound on the computer. Adam will read the finished text, using word-matching games and look–cover–write–check method for problem words.	The book will be completed and Adam will read it to his class.	January 1996: Book completed. Still not keen to write but enjoys coming to me. He was very pleased with his book and read it out during a Y7 assembly.
Adam will spell these words correctly, from dictation: brake, lever, pads, speed.	He will compile a wordsearch incorporating these words. He will look at other words in the 'ee' family and the 'ake' family.	Adam will correctly spell 'ee' and 'ake' words from dictation and in his free writing.	12 January 1996: 1 spelling right. 25 January 1996: All spellings right.

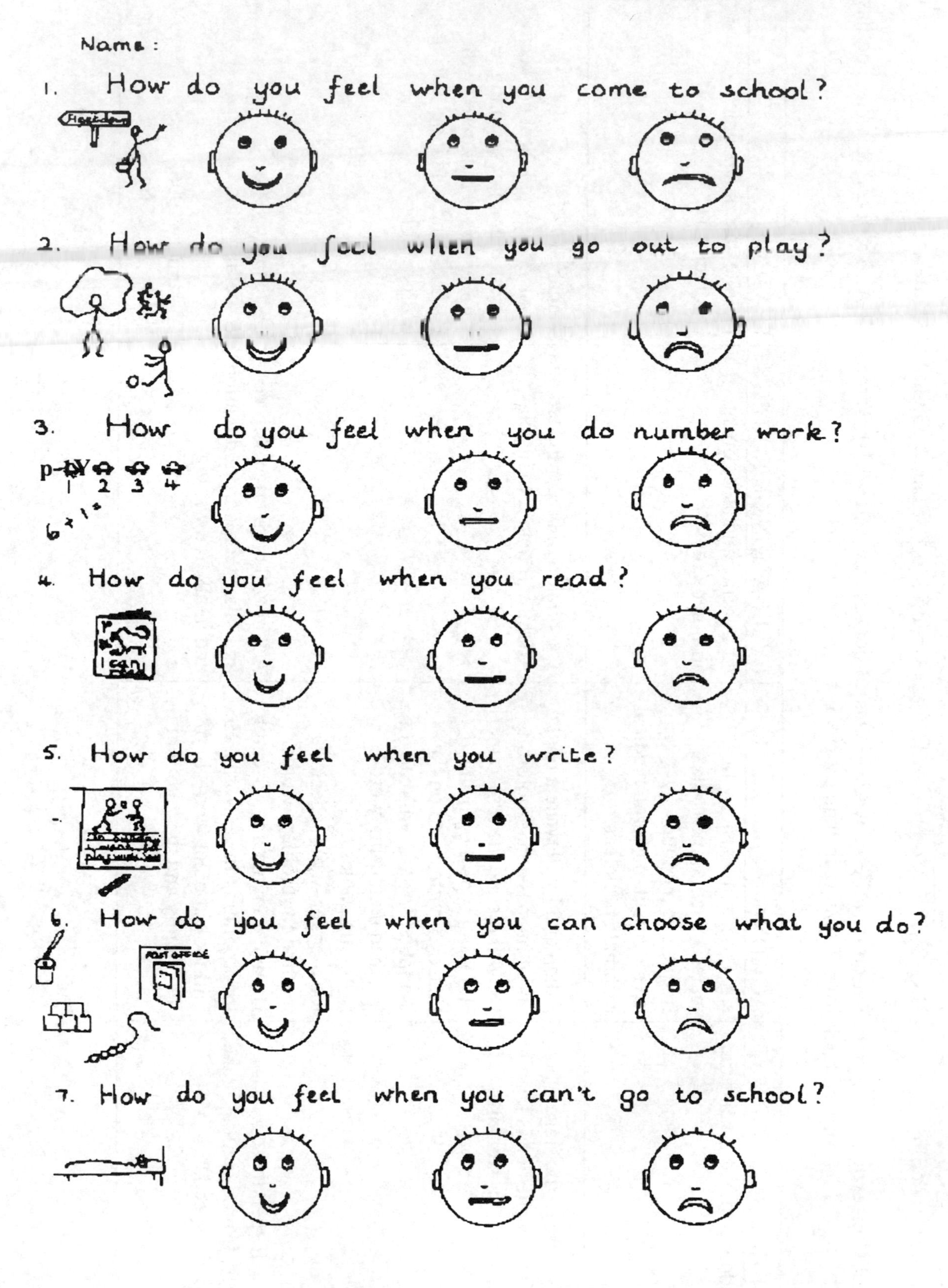

Name :

1. How do you feel when you come to school?

2. How do you feel when you go out to play?

3. How do you feel when you do number work?

4. How do you feel when you read?

5. How do you feel when you write?

6. How do you feel when you can choose what you do?

7. How do you feel when you can't go to school?

DAILY MONITORING PROFORMA

PERSON RESPONSIBLE AND PURPOSE OF MONITORING	General questions asked by the person who delivers the IEP concerning the child's response to his/her IEP	Task Possible action	Strategy resource Possible action	Setting/Context Possible action

Resources for peer support

Bliss, T. and Robinson, G. (1995) *Developing Circle Time.* Lucky Duck Publications.

Curry, M. and Broomfield, C. (1994) *Personal and Social Education for Primary Schools through Circle Time.* NASEN Enterprises Ltd.

McNamara, S. and Moreton, G. (1995) *Changing Behaviour: Teaching Children with Emotional and Behavioural Difficulties in Primary and Secondary Classrooms.* David Fulton.

Moseley, J. (1993) *Turn Your School Around.* Wisbech: LDA.

Moseley, J. (1996) *Quality Circle Time in the Primary School.* Wisbech LDA.

Circle of Friends Publisher's Web Site
http://www.inclusion.com/tools.Circles.html

Circle of Inclusion Project Web Site
http://circleofinclusion.org/

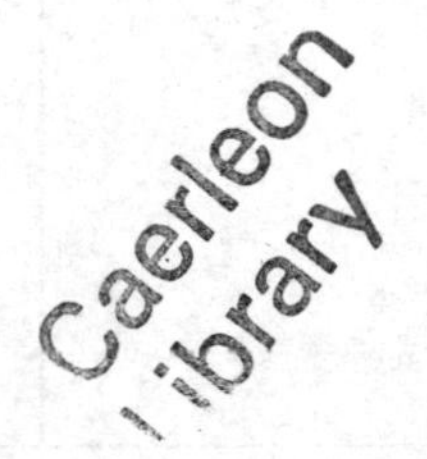